# Fasts and Festivals

## Worship Resources for the Liturgical Year

### Michael Forster

Kevin
Mayhew

First published in 1994 by
KEVIN MAYHEW LTD
Rattlesden
Bury St Edmunds
Suffolk IP30 0SZ

The publishers wish to express their gratitude
to the following:

Inmates of H M Prison, Leicester for prayers written for a chapel mission.
Used by permission of the Chaplain.

The Baptist Union of Great Britain for permission to use
an extract from *Patterns and Prayers for Christian Worship*.

ICOREC, for permission to use an extract from *Advent and Ecology*
by Martin Palmer, published by WWF/BBC, 1988.

Jan Berry for permission to use God of Creation
from *Bread of Tomorrow* ed J Morley, (SPCK).

Jubilate Hymns for permission to use
*Spirit of the Living God*, © Michael Baughen/Jubilate Hymns.

The Division of Christian Education of the National Council of the Churches
of Christ in the USA for extracts from the New Revised Standard Version
of the Bible, copyright 1989.

ISBN 086209 487 9

Front Cover: *Seven Saints* by Fra Filippo Lippi (1406-1469).
Reproduced by courtesy of the Trustees, The National Gallery, London


Typesetting & Page Creation by Anne Haskell
Cover Design by Graham Johnstone
Printed and bound in Great Britain.

# CONTENTS

# FOREWORD

THIS BOOK, like its prequel, *High Days and Holy Days*, is intended as a resource for anyone responsible for leading worship on special occasions in the Christian year. As before, the Advent and Lent ceremonies (this time based on ASB Year Two) are designed to be slotted into the regular weekly worship, while the other services are complete in themselves, and are not connected specifically with the lectionary.

Again, flexibility is the key-word. The fully-scripted services can be used as they stand, with minimal preparation, or different elements can be lifted out and used as ministers see fit. In the former case, they will relieve the pressure – particularly in churches without the services of a full-time minister – at busy times in the year.

I have found the use of dialogues in worship to be very effective. The frequent change of voice, and the individual style each reader brings, makes listening much easier for the congregation, and also involves more people in the active leading of worship.

Both this book and its prequel have arisen out of the worship of an actual congregation. On the one hand, this means that most of the material (there has necessarily been some adaptation) is tried and tested. On the other, it may well be necessary to make minor adjustments, in order to make the best use of the services elsewhere. They are offered in the hope that they may not only facilitate but also encourage the further development of worship.

MICHAEL FORSTER

# ADVENT CANDLE CEREMONIES

## The Light Shines in the Darkness

THESE ADVENT Candle ceremonies use the themes and readings from the ASB lectionary, Year Two, and are intended to be slotted into the normal Sunday service, with whatever adjustments may be necessary to the normal pattern.

Sometimes only one reading is actually used in the ceremony, and care must therefore be taken in the preparation of the whole service, to ensure a proper balance of readings.

The aim is to look for signs of the light shining in the darkness in the world around, throughout the Advent season. Each week, the congregation is given the opportunity of taking some small action to enable the light to shine more brightly. You will need to prepare in advance:

**An Advent Crown** with five candles.

**An Advent Calendar.** This has five windows, and could represent the windows of the church, opening out onto the surrounding world. When opened, the windows show representations of the following.

| | |
|---|---|
| Advent 1 | Mental health issues |
| Advent 2 | Prisons |
| Advent 3 | International injustice |
| Advent 4 | Homelessness |
| Christmas | Light |

It might be helpful to reproduce the pictures in larger form on OHP acetates. It is also important to make contact in advance, at least with a local mental health or learning disability unit – so that the necessary practical arrangements can be made. It goes without saying, of course, that this must be done with the utmost sensitivity and respect.

**Christmas Cards**, produced by the children of the church and, if applicable, associated organisations, for use on Advent Sunday. In our case, the staff at a local hospital were given the cards in advance, wrote on each the first name of a resident, and returned them to us. So enthusiastic had the children been that each resident received a good number of cards. Any not signed after the service were collected by a small group of people, signed and put with the rest. So all the cards were used.

**A petition** for signing on Advent 4, calling on the government to make and encourage better housing provision. The precise details of this will depend on the prevailing circumstances at the time, but organisations such as Shelter or the Churches' National Housing Coalition should be able and willing to help.

These preparations offer a good opportunity to utilise the creative skills of a number of people.

When these ceremonies were used, special speakers were invited, wherever possible, to help open up the particular subject of each week. These included a resident and member of staff from the local hospital to which cards were being sent, and someone involved in providing accommodation for homeless people.

| | |
|---|---|
| *Reader* | Hear the word of God. <br> Isaiah 51:4-11 |
| *Voice 1* | *(gloomily)* Well, it'll soon be Christmas. . . |
| *Voice 2* | Jesus coming into the world . . . |
| *Voice 3* | Light shining in the darkness . . . |
| *Voice 1* | Oh, that's just words. Most people haven't got a clue about 'God with us' and all that light in the darkness stuff – they're only interested in having a good time. |
| *Voice 2* | O.K. – let's help them a bit – let's use Advent to point to where God is already coming into the world. Matthew 25 says we'll find him among the poor, the embarrassing and the unwanted. And when we show kindness to them, we're really doing it for him. |
| *Voice 1* | Well, there are plenty of those around. Perhaps we could shine a little light into their darkness this Advent. |
| *Voice 3* | Yes, but it's more than that. If Christ is there, then there already is light in those places. Our job is to point it out, and help it to shine a little more brightly. |
| *Voice 2* | Tell you what – why don't we listen to what they want to say, and try to understand them. Perhaps we might see Christ in a new way, as well. |
| *Voice 1* | That's all very well, but how will we know where to start? I mean, who are those people around here? |
| *Voice 3* | Well, if we open the windows and look out to our community, we might see some interesting examples. |
| | *A child opens the first window of the Advent Calendar.* |
| *Voice 2* | People with learning disability often get pushed out – partly because of a lack of confidence on our part. But today we make a special effort to give them a little care. |
| *Voice 1* | I don't see how we can do that – you need qualifications and things. |
| *Voice 3* | Not to send a Christmas card, you don't. A lot of mentally disabled people are very lonely and neglected. So the children of the church have made some cards to send to residents at a local hospital. All we've got to do is sign them, and put them in the box to be delivered there. |
| *Voice 1* | That's not much! |
| *Voice 3* | No, but it's a lot more than nothing. It's easy for us, and it will mean so much to them. Tell you what: why don't we all do it? |
| *Voice 2* | The cards are at the back of the church. If you wish to take part in this, please sign one and leave it in the box on the table. The cards will be delivered in time for Christmas. |

| | |
|---|---|
| *Reader* | Hear the gospel of Christ. |
| | Matthew 25:31-46 |
| | *A child lights one candle.* |
| *Minister* | The light shines in the darkness. |
| *All* | And the darkness has not overcome it. |
| *Minister* | We sing the first verse of the carol: From God goes forth the light of truth. *(See Appendix)* |

# SECOND SUNDAY IN ADVENT

*Reader*    Hear the gospel of Christ.
Luke 4:14-21

*Voice 1*    If, as Jesus said, that scripture has already come true, then we should be able to see those things happening today – captives being freed, sick healed, and so on.

*Voice 2*    Well we can. All over the world there are people –

*Voice 1*    *(Interrupting)* I'm not talking about all over the world.
We should be able to see it actually happening here.

*Voice 3*    Let's open another window and look out – you never know what we might see.

*A child opens the second window of the Advent Calendar.*

*Voice 1*    Prisons. I've heard about prisons – there's not much light in the darkness there.

*Voice 2*    That's not necessarily true, actually. If you want an example, listen to this poem by an inmate at Leicester Prison.

*Reader*    I can't make you love me,
   I don't want to try.
I can't make you happy,
   I can't make you cry.
I can't stop you fighting,
   I can't interfere;
although wars are frightening,
   I can't stop your fear.
I gave you free will,
   just like my own,
to love or to kill,
   together or alone.
I gave you my Son
   to show you the way,
so we could be one
   some day.
I'm here when you're able,
   my patience is strong;
here's food at the table
   where my children belong.
Lonely is a God
   without his creation;
just put down the rod
   and live in my nation.

*Voice 3*    Now there's someone who has found some real light in prison.

10

| | |
|---|---|
| *Voice 2* | Wouldn't it be wonderful if we could help the light to glow a little brighter this Christmas! |
| *Voice 3* | Well, we've already done something – we've listened to them. And we can pray with them. |
| *Voice 1* | You mean pray *for* them |
| *Voice 3* | No, I mean *with* them. Instead of using our words, we'll use theirs. |
| *Voice 1* | That's not much! |
| *Voice 3* | No, but it's a lot more than nothing. It's easy for us, and it will mean so much to them. Tell you what: why don't we all do it? |
| *Reader* | Let us pray with the inmates of the prison: |

**PRAYERS WRITTEN BY INMATES**

WE PRAY WITH AND FOR THEM USING THEIR OWN WORDS.

| | |
|---|---|
| *All* | Our heavenly Father: We praise and thank you for this time together, and we pray today that you will hear us. We come to you knowing that you are a loving God, who forgives our many sins. We all thank you for sending your Jesus whom we sincerely love. Father, we bring the Middle East to you and we pray that the people who are involved will do your will, in Jesus' name. Amen |
| *All* | Dear God, thanks for the world we live in. Thanks for the food we eat and thanks for my friends. Amen |
| | *A child lights two candles.* |
| *Minister* | The light shines in the darkness. |
| *All* | And the darkness has not overcome it. |
| *Minister* | We sing the first two verses of the carol: From God goes forth the light of truth. *(See Appendix)* |

# THIRD SUNDAY IN ADVENT

*Voice 1*   You know, it's all very well, what we've been doing, but I can't help thinking that it's rather futile – I mean, the world's so full of problems. All we can do is scratch the surface.

*Voice 2*   But the world's also full of people who are doing just that. And the message of the Gospel is that scratching makes a difference.

*Voice 3*   That's right. Jesus said that wherever people are being helped it's a sign that God is at work.

*Voice 2*   John expected great upheavals and revolutions, but Jesus pointed him to smaller things

*Reader*   Hear the gospel of Christ.
Matthew 11:2-6

*Voice 1*   That's all very well, and we've seen something of that happening here. But it's time to look a bit further afield. It's about time we opened another window.

*A child opens the third window of the Advent Calendar.*

*Voice 1*   There, you see – there's a great big world out there, with enormous problems. What on earth can we do?

*Voice 2*   We could support Amnesty International. Over the years, they have mobilised thousands of people to support prisoners of conscience,

*Voice 3*   got prisoners released,

*Voice 2*   saved people from torture,

*Voice 3*   campaigned for justice in all parts of the world.

*Voice 2*   That's an awful lot of surface-scratching!

*Voice 3*   So that's what we could do – we could make a donation to Amnesty. Then we'd know we'd done something to make the world a little less unjust.

*Voice 1*   That's a great idea. There's a plate on the table at the back for any contributions you may want to make. This is a good way of helping those words of Jesus to come true:

*Reader*   The blind receive their sight, the lame walk, the lepers are cleansed, the deaf hear, the dead are raised, and the poor have good news brought to them.

*A child lights three candles.*

*Minister*   The light shines in the darkness.

*All*   And the darkness has not overcome it.

*Minister*   We sing the first three verses of the carol: From God goes forth the light of truth. *(See Appendix)*

# FOURTH SUNDAY IN ADVENT

| | |
|---|---|
| *Minister* | We hear two readings from Scripture. |
| *Reader* | Hear the word of God.<br>Zechariah 2: 10 - end<br>Matthew 1:18-23 |
| | *A child opens the fourth window of the Advent Calendar* |
| *Voice 1* | That stuff in the readings is all very well – but what does it mean to talk about God coming to live in creation, to people who have got nowhere to live themselves? |
| *Voice 2* | Zechariah speaks about God coming to live among his people, wherever they are. So the Christmas message of 'God with us' is still for them. |
| *Voice 1* | Yes, but it's not really a great deal of help, when you're freezing to death, for someone from a nice warm home to tell you that God is with you! |
| *Voice 3* | Well, in that case we've got to do something positive – get to the heart of the problem. |
| *Voice 1* | The heart of the problem is that people have no homes.<br>We can't do anything about that. |
| *Voice 2* | No, but we know someone who can. People not having homes is the result – not the cause of the problem. That goes much deeper, and a significant part of it is government policy. If we could change that policy, we'd make a real difference. |
| *Voice 1* | Fat chance we've got of doing that! |
| *Voice 2* | It wouldn't be the first time a British government had changed its mind because of public pressure. and it wouldn't be the first time a local church had been involved in that. |
| *Voice 3* | That's right. It's worked in the past – at least we could give it a try. |
| *Voice 2* | On the table at the back of the church is a politely-worded letter to the Secretary of State for the Environment, asking the Government to allow and encourage the provision of more council housing. |
| *Voice 3* | So all we have to do is sign it before we leave the building.<br>That sounds easy enough |
| *Voice 1* | Tell you what, why don't we all do it? |
| | *A child lights four candles.* |
| *Minister* | The light shines in the darkness. |
| *All* | And the darkness has not overcome it. |
| *Minister* | We sing the first four verses of the carol: From God goes forth the light of truth. *(See Appendix)* |

# Christmas Day

*A child opens the final window of the Advent Calendar*

**Reader**   The light shines in the darkness, and the darkness has not overcome it.

**Voice 1**   Jesus coming into the world was just like a light being lit in a dark place. Lots of people found new hope, new love and new life because of him.

**Voice 2**   During Advent, we've been looking around us, and we've found a number of dark places where the light is shining, showing that God is living in the world.

**Voice 3**   And each week, we've done something to try and help the light to shine more brightly.

## Review: 'The Four Weeks of Advent'

**Voice 1**   In the first week of Advent, we heard about mentally disabled people, and those who work with them.

**Voice 2**   And we sent them some Christmas Cards, which the children of the Church had made.

*A child lights one candle.*

**Minister**   The light shines in the darkness.

**All**   And the darkness has not overcome it.

**Voice 1**   In the second week of Advent, we heard about people in prison – who are too easily forgotten or undervalued.

**Voice 2**   And we made a point of listening to their thoughts.

**Voice 3**   And praying their prayers.

*A child lights one candle.*

**Minister**   The light shines in the darkness.

**All**   And the darkness has not overcome it.

**Voice 1**   In the third week of Advent, we heard about the poverty in the Third World, and how some people are working to relieve it.

**Voice 3**   And we sent a donation to Amnesty International, who try to protect prisoners of conscience.

*A child lights one candle.*

**Minister**   The light shines in the darkness.

**All**   And the darkness has not overcome it.

**Voice 1**   In the Fourth week of Advent, we thought about homeless people.

**Voice 2**   And we signed a letter to [Name],

**Voice 3**   Secretary of State for the Environment,

**Voice 2**   Asking her/him to help provide more housing.

*A child lights one candle.*

| | |
|---|---|
| *Minister* | The light shines in the darkness. |
| *All* | And the darkness has not overcome it. |
| *Minister* | Soon we're going to light the Christmas Candle, but first we hear the story of how light came into the world in Jesus. |
| *Reader* | Hear the gospel of Christ.<br>Luke 2:1-14 |

*A child lights the final candle.*

| | |
|---|---|
| *Minister* | The light shines in the darkness. |
| *All* | And the darkness has not overcome it. |
| *Minister* | We sing the carol: From God goes forth the light of truth.<br>*(See Appendix)* |

Minister    A small flame is offered.
Minister    The light shines in the darkness
All          And the darkness has not overcome it
Minister    Soon we're going to light the Christmas Candle, but first we hear the story of how light came into the world in Jesus.
Reader      Hear the gospel of Christ.
            Luke 2:1–...

            A small lights the past can lie
Minister    The light shines in the darkness
All          And the darkness has not overcome it
Minister    We sing the carol 'From God goes forth the light of truth'
            (We sing...)

# NATIVITY SERVICE

THE MAIN part of this service is quite traditional, consisting of hymns and readings during which the familiar story can be mimed by the children in the time-honoured way. Then a dialogue takes place between two people, posing the question, 'Where can we find Jesus now?' This is addressed through a short presentation based on Matthew 25: 31-40.

# Order of Service

WELCOME

Welcome to this Nativity Service. Mostly, it will follow the traditional pattern, using readings and hymns and, during the readings, the children will act out the story. After that has happened, we shall pose the question, 'Where is Jesus to be found now?' We believe the bible shows us how we can find Jesus and offer him gifts in our own place and time. This story is not only about something which happened long ago, but is about something which is still happening now, and we are called not only to this very attractive crib, but to other places, perhaps rather less pretty but much more real. We shall pursue that idea further towards the end of the service. Now, let us pray.

PRAYER OF ADORATION

Eternal God, we come before you in adoration. We do not adore a baby in a manger, safely locked into an earlier age and made innocuous by tradition. Rather we adore you as you are, and as this event has revealed you: a God of humility and love, coming to us in the unexpected. We thank you for the assurance of your presence in those parts of life that are not beautiful or romantic, and we pray that through this traditional scene, you will turn our hearts and minds to the world in which you still come to us. Turn upside down our ideas about power and glory, and show us the true glory of self-giving love, through Jesus Christ our Lord. Amen.

PRAYER OF CONFESSION

Jesus, born among the homeless to live among the poor, calling to your side and to your manger those whom society did not want – the dirty, sick, the despised, and the simply different, forgive us for failing to notice you at this time of year – for seeking happiness in excessive indulgence rather than in serving you. Call us back to yourself, in the service of the poor, and there let us find true salvation, through Jesus Christ our Lord. Amen.

ASSURANCE OF FORGIVENESS

God so loved the world that he gave his one and only Son, that whoever believes in him shall not perish but have eternal life.                    *John 3:16*

HYMN          Lord Jesus Christ
              *or* Let all mortal flesh keep silence

READING       Isaiah 9:2,6,7

HYMN          Hail to the Lord's Anointed
              *or* Hark! The herald angels sing

READING       Luke 1:26-38,46-56

| HYMN | Tell out, my soul, the greatness of the Lord |
|------|----------------------------------------------|
| | *or* A great and mighty wonder |

| READING | Luke 2:1-7 |
|---------|------------|

| HYMN | O little town |
|------|---------------|
| | *or* Child in the manger |

| READING | Luke 2:8-18 |
|---------|-------------|

| HYMN | See amid the winter's snow |
|------|----------------------------|
| | *or* While shepherds watched |

| READING | Matthew 2:1-11 |
|---------|----------------|

| HYMN | The first nowell |
|------|------------------|
| | *or* As with gladness |

OFFERTORY

| HYMN | Mary, blessed teenage mother *(see Appendix)* |
|------|------------------------------------------------|
| | *or* Unto us a boy is born |

FIRST DIALOGUE

*Voice 1*  I wonder why so few people recognised who Jesus was. I mean, where were the religious people – the priests and the pharisees?

*Voice 2*  I suppose they were expecting something a bit different. They expected a traditional kind of king – all power and posh clothes.

*Voice 1*  So, what's wrong with that – isn't God supposed to be powerful?

*Voice 2*  Somebody hasn't been reading her/his bible! No-one's saying God isn't powerful – but all through the Old Testament, he had been trying to change people's understanding of what power actually meant.

*Voice 1*  So how does a baby in a manger help with that?

*Voice 2*  On its own, perhaps not very much. But you must not separate Jesus's birth from the rest of his life. The point is that he started as he meant to go on. For him, power had to go with humility, and leadership had to be expressed in loving service.

*Voice 1*  So all this is supposed to change our ideas of power and authority –– to teach us that humility is not the same as weakness, and humble service is the highest form of leadership.

*Voice 2*  I do believe s/he's got it!

HYMN    The Servant King

SECOND DIALOGUE

Voice 1    So Jesus came just to be an example to us. Well, it didn't work,
did it? After all, how many servant kings do you know?
People don't seem to have learnt anything at all.

Voice 2    No, he did *not* come just to be an example. The point is that he's
always here, and like those people in the stories,
we are invited to join him.

Voice 1    That's all very well, but the shepherds and the wise men had a
manger to go to – not to mention a few heavenly bodies to show
them the way! It's harder for us – where do we start to look?

Voice 2    Well, start by telling me some of the problems Jesus had
when he was born.

Voice 1    Well, he was homeless – and King Herod was after his blood . . .

Voice 2    And what about when he was older?

Voice 1    He was homeless then, wasn't he? And he always seemed to be
in the wrong sort of company: bad people, dirty people,
unreliable people, down-and-out people . . .

Voice 2    So where do you think he is now? Where are you going to start
looking for him?

Voice 1    Well, according to that, I suppose in the places no-one wants
to go, among the people no-one wants to see.

Voice 1    I do believe s/he's got it!

READING    Matthew 25: 31-40

*As this passage is read, a short mime illustrates each example:*

'hungry'    A child enters from one side, looking dejected.
Another child meets the first and hands over a loaf of bread.
Both children dance off together.

'thirsty'    As above, but with a tumbler representing a glass of water.

'stranger'    A child enters, gazing around in bewilderment
and consulting a street map. The second child enters,
they join hands and leave together.

'naked'    A child enters wearing only gym shorts and singlet,
and obviously cold. A second child meets the first, wraps a
blanket around the shoulders and they leave together.

'sick'    A child enters, limping, and the second meets and offers
support as they leave together.

'in prison' Two children enter, 'police' and 'prisoner.'
A second child enters and extends a hand to the 'prisoner'.
All three leave together.

PRAYERS OF INTERCESSION

In the presence of the vulnerable infant Christ, let us pray for all who are obsessed with power, all who abuse it, and all who suffer because of its misuse.

*Silence*

Christ, call us to serve you,
**in the world of today.**

In the presence of the homeless Christ, let us pray for all who are denied homes, whether by personal difficulties, social barriers or government policies.

*Silence*

Christ, call us to serve you,
**in the world of today.**

In the presence of the Jewish Christ, let us pray for all who suffer because of religious or racial prejudice.

*Silence*

Christ, call us to serve you,
**in the world of today.**

In the presence of the dependent Christ, let us pray for ourselves, for faith to relinquish ourselves into others' hands, that we may experience love.

*Silence*

Christ, call us to serve you,
**in the world of today.**

Holy God, fill our lives with light, with love, but most of all with compassion. And give us time for those for whom the world has none, through Jesus Christ our Lord. Amen.

HYMN       O come, all ye faithful

BENEDICTION

# LENT VIGIL CEREMONIES

## Watch and Pray

L ENT, like Advent, is a time of preparation for a great festival. So it seems appropriate to adapt the Advent ideas for this season. As with Advent, the Lent ceremonies, which fit with the readings in the ASB lectionary, are not complete in themselves, but are designed to be fitted into the normal order of service, which may need to be slightly adapted. The material has been arranged as suits the occasion, from week to week. Sometimes both readings are used, and sometimes only one. Careful preparation of the whole service will be needed to make the best use of these ceremonies.

The atmosphere in Lent needs to be a little different, and so the word 'vigil' has been used. The candle may symbolise the watchman's fire as we obey Christ's injunction to the disciples to watch and pray with him.

It is suggested that only one candle is used – perhaps a large one bearing a suitable symbol. Alternatively, a pillar candle could be surrounded with barbed wire, as in the logo of Amnesty International. Then, in the intercessions elsewhere in the services, a special point could be made of being alongside those who watch and pray for justice.

The vigils focus upon the temptations of Christ, and try to explore the ways in which those temptations are still presented to the church today. Three of the voices represent the temptations, and this will be clearer if the same four people are available to read the main parts each week throughout Lent.

As in Advent, the use of a 'calendar' is suggested, although it is not indispensable, to illustrate visually the main point for each week. This could well be done with OHP slides, again utilising the gifts of other members of the congregation.

Finally, the presentation will be more effective if the people reading Voices One to Three stand as a group, slightly apart from Voice Four who confronts them.

*A child opens the first window of the Lent Calendar.*

| | |
|---|---|
| Minister | These are difficult days for any church. How do we get people to listen to our message? Where do we begin? Jesus went away to think about those things, and someone else had some suggestions for him. What do we make of those suggestions, now? |
| Voice 1 | The first priority is survival. If the church doesn't survive it can't continue its mission – and with all the expenses of today, you've got to think about practical things, like money. But you're people of faith. So why not call on God for a miracle? If you really had faith, and really prayed hard, surely God would send you the money. |
| Voice 4 | It's a tempting idea, but Jesus said there are more important things. So, precisely because we *do* have faith, we'll devote our prayers to other things – or rather, to other people. |
| Voice 2 | Well, if you're not prepared to pray for money, then you'd better start being a bit more practical. What about the money you give away? If you cut that out, you'd be better off. Why not rent the hall to the National Front? And what about some really hard-hitting preaching on tithing? Guilt is a very good loosener of purse-strings. I could give you the world, if only you'd listen to me! |
| Voice 4 | And that's just what we're not going to do. The church would cease to be the church if it just adopted all the ways of the world, without a thought for what is right. |
| Voice 3 | Well, there is one other possibility: do something spectacular – draw the crowds. If you really have faith, you should be able to arrange something to get the punters coming. And if you can't, then I can. People really love spectacle – so give them a little excitement. |
| Voice 4 | What you're really saying is that we should use God for our own ends. All this is nothing to do with the kingdom of God, and you know it. No, we shall stay true to the gospel of love. We're here to serve people, not exploit them – even if they don't appreciate it. |
| Voice 1 | Well, we're not getting anywhere here. But not to worry; there'll be other opportunities. Let's just bide our time. |
| Reader | Hear the word of God. Luke 4:1-13 |

*A child lights the candle.*

| | |
|---|---|
| Minister | Watch and pray |
| All | Lest we fall into temptation. |
| Minister | We remain seated and sing, as a prayer, the first verse of the hymn: Keep watch and pray. *(See Appendix)* |

# Second Sunday in Lent

*A child opens the second window of the Lent Calendar.*

| | |
|---|---|
| *Minister* | We see Jesus disputing with the Pharisees, who are trying to say that he is not what he seems. |
| *Voice 1* | One of the problems with the church is that it's too humble. You've got to get back to the idea that only the church is right, and everyone else is wrong. |
| *Voice 4* | We can't say that, because it's not true. You've only got to look to see that there's good outside of the church – not to mention the bad that's on the inside! |
| *Voice 2* | Well, there's no need to admit it. Do what the pharisees did with Jesus: just keep the outward appearance convincing, and find ways to explain away anything good that happens outside. Say it's the work of the devil, or that they're doing the right things for the wrong reasons. |
| *Voice 4* | You're right to say that that's what the pharisees tried to do. They tried never to admit that there was anything good in Jesus. But Jesus always saw good in people of other traditions. He even saw good in the pharisees! |
| *Voice 3* | That's all very well, but you won't fill the church by saying good things about the opposition. |
| *Voice 4* | Filling the church is not the priority. Truth and integrity are the priorities. Jesus recognised faith in people who were not even Jews, and affirmed the healing work of someone who was not part of his group. So if the Holy Spirit sees fit to use people we don't happen to agree with, we must not slander him by claiming that good is evil. |
| *Reader* | Hear the word of God Matthew 12:22-32 |

*A child lights the candle.*

| | |
|---|---|
| *Minister* | Watch and pray |
| *All* | Lest we fall into temptation. |
| *Minister* | We remain seated and sing, as a prayer, the first two verses of the hymn: Keep watch and pray. *(See Appendix)* |

# THIRD SUNDAY IN LENT

*A child opens the third window of the Lent Calendar.*

| | |
|---|---|
| Minister | Peter recognises Jesus as the Messiah, but it becomes clear that he still has a very mistaken idea of what kind of messiah Jesus is to be. |
| Voice 2 | The trouble today is that Jesus is not glorified enough. People say all kinds of things about him – and some of them are quite scandalous – and too often the church does not seem to defend him. |
| Voice 4 | But Jesus himself said that he was going to be humiliated – and he didn't try to defend himself. He also said that, if that were the right course, he could do it perfectly well for himself without our help, anyway – but he chooses not to. |
| Voice 1 | That's all very well, but you have to think about your own position. It's not just a case of protecting Jesus; if people attack him and get away with it, then you're vulnerable as well. |
| Voice 4 | That's what it's really about, isn't it? When we rush to protect Jesus, it's ourselves we're really concerned about. We know that we're called to share his pain with him, and that's not a very attractive prospect. So we say we're protecting him, but often it's really our own reputations and pride we're concerned about. |
| Voice 3 | You can rationalise all you like, but how are you going to draw the crowds in on that kind of basis? |
| Voice 4 | Well, is it actually about that? The only crowds that Jesus drew were not worth drawing, anyway. Our job is not to enshrine Jesus and call people in to look at him, but to join him where he already is – among the other misunderstood, misrepresented and persecuted people. That's what the gospel seems to say to me. |
| Reader | Hear the word of God<br>Matthew 16:13-28 |

*A child lights the candle.*

| | |
|---|---|
| Minister | Watch and pray |
| All | Lest we fall into temptation. |
| Minister | We remain seated and sing, as a prayer, the first three verses of the hymn: Keep watch and pray. *(See Appendix)* |

# FOURTH SUNDAY IN LENT

*A child opens the fourth window of the Lent Calendar.*

**Minister**  The transfiguration, about which we shall read in a moment,
was a very exciting experience. It was also very secure – all the most
important people were there, and the harsh world was
a long way away. Small wonder that Peter wanted to stay there.

**Voice 1**  This is a nice building, isn't it? It's warm, the chairs are comfortable –
why not stay here? Mission and outreach are all very well,
but it's a dog-eat-dog world out there. So forget the community
involvement; let's stay here.

**Voice 4**  This place is important, yes – but it's a place from which to go out.
You're right in saying it's a harsh world out there, but that's where
God chooses to be. The gospel speaks of him 'pitching his tent' among
the people – not on some mountain top, away from them.
So that's where we've got to be.

**Voice 2**  The trouble with that is that you never know who you're going to
have to meet out there. In here, you know you're only going to get
the right sort of people. After all, the transfiguration was for the
select few.

**Voice 4**  Jesus spent the whole of his ministry mixing with the 'wrong' people,
and he also told us that that's where we shall find him.
So we're going to look.

**Voice 3**  Of course, the alternative is to get them into here. You don't need to
do any of that community-involvement stuff. Just promise them a
good time. Tell them that Christians are always happy, because Jesus
protects them from pain and makes them prosper. That'll get them in!

**Voice 4**  And then what do we tell them about the cross? The gospel is of new
life through death – hope from within pain. There's nothing there
about pain-avoidance. What we need to say is that God is present and
active in the Gethsemanes and Calvaries of life. And the only way to
say that convincingly is to be there. So we're going to go to where
people are and speak of hope there. We're going back down from the
mountain. That's what the first disciples had to do.

**Reader**  Hear the word of God.
Matthew 17:1-13

*A child lights the candle.*

**Minister**  Watch and pray

**All**  Lest we fall into temptation.

**Minister**  We remain seated and sing, as a prayer, the first four verses
of the hymn: Keep watch and pray. *(See Appendix)*

# Fifth Sunday in Lent

*A child opens the fifth window of the Lent Calendar.*

Minister    On the road to Jerusalem, Jesus told his disciples again how he was going to suffer. But at least two of the disciples weren't listening. They were more concerned with their own status. The same temptation is there for the church of today.

Voice 1    People don't want all this 'humble and meek' stuff. What makes the world go round is power. Everyone knows that God looks after his own – or at least, that's what they want to know. Why not just tell them what they want to hear?

Voice 4    I don't remember Jesus saying that that was our job. The whole reason he was crucified was that he wouldn't just tell people what they wanted him to tell them – and that included his disciples.

Voice 2    But there was a time when being a Christian was a mark of respectability. You meant something – people looked up to you. There doesn't seem to be much percentage in it these days, though.

Voice 4    Jesus always said that the 'percentage' was in doing the will of God. You don't become a Christian in order to be looked up to – it has its own rewards, which are quite different.

Voice 3    But people want a powerful church – you might say they need it. They'll come to a church like that.

Voice 4    Well, I've said before that pulling in the crowds is not our job. But as far as power is concerned, don't we believe there is power in the cross? The church is never more powerful than when it is serving others – never more glorious than when it stands with the people society rejects.

Reader    Hear what Jesus says about power and leadership.
Mark 10:32-45

*A child lights the candle.*

Minister    Watch and pray

All    Lest we fall into temptation.

Minister    We remain seated and sing, as a prayer, the first five verses of the hymn: Keep watch and pray. (*See Appendix*)

# PALM SUNDAY

*A child opens the sixth window of the Lent Calendar.*

| | |
|---|---|
| Minister | Palm Sunday: Jesus risked everything to confront the world with the gospel, but he was just as misunderstood then as he always had been. |
| Voice 1 | It's a costly business, religion. Can't we do it on a kind of part-time basis? Putting God first, and changing the world and all that, is all very well, but you have to keep it in proportion. |
| Voice 4 | Well, Jesus's 'proportion' was that he gave everything. He didn't want to change the world a little – he wanted to change it completely – even if it cost him his life. There are more important things than our own comfort. |
| Voice 2 | Well, if the church wants to change the world, it will need to play the world at its own game. It's all about power. The church needs to get into the revolution business. |
| Voice 4 | If Jesus had wanted to do that, he'd have ridden into Jerusalem on a horse – not a donkey. He wanted to present an alternative to the world's ways – not descend to them himself. And if we're his people, then we have to do things in his way, and not the world's. |
| Voice 3 | Well, you have to admit it got the crowds going. Once you've got people roused up, you can do anything. |
| Voice 4 | But the trouble is it didn't last. They were shouting 'Hosanna!' on Palm Sunday and 'Crucify him!' by Friday! If that's what populism does, we can manage without it, thank you very much. |
| Reader | Hear the word of God<br>Matthew 21:1-13 |

*A child lights the candle.*

| | |
|---|---|
| Minister | Watch and pray |
| All | Lest we fall into temptation. |
| Minister | We remain seated and sing, as a prayer, the first six verses of the hymn: Keep watch and pray. *(See Appendix)* |

# GOOD FRIDAY

*A child opens the seventh window of the Lent Calendar.*

Voice 1    (*angrily*) There – that's what happens when you put others first.
All the way through, I told him, 'Look after Number One', but would
he listen? All he ever wanted to do was help other people. From the
time he refused to turn stones into bread – as if that would have done
any harm – the writing was on the wall.

Voice 2    Even then, he could have saved himself. Just a little compromise here
and there – that's all it needed. That's the way the world works,
but he never understood that. I told him that if he did things my way
he could have had everything. But he cared more about his precious
integrity than his life.

Voice 3    It's not too late, though. If he's who he says he is, he can just come
down from the cross. That would really show them! I said at the start
he needed a gimmick. If he came down from the cross now, he'd have
the people in the palm of his hand!

Voice 4    Father, forgive them: they don't know what they are saying.

They still need to learn how different your ways are from the world's.
Everyone likes to see spectacular things happening; they still have to
learn about patience and faith. But they will.

Father, forgive them: they don't know what they are saying.

Reader    We hear the story of the crucifixion.
John 19:1-37

*A child lights the candle.*

Minister    Watch and pray

All    Lest we fall into temptation.

Minister    We stand and sing the hymn: Keep watch and pray. (*See Appendix*)

# GOOD FRIDAY SERVICE

## The Way of the Cross

THIS SERVICE is not specifically related to the Lent Vigils. In those churches which have two services on Good Friday, the Lent Vigil could be included in the morning service, and this order used in the evening.

This service uses the crucifixion to focus on God's presence in places where life is painful. What does it mean for us to stand with the crucified Christ in the present day world? And can we do it in a way which does not involve some degree of suffering for us? What does it mean to 'walk the way of the cross'?

The congregation is invited, for the main part of the service, to do just that. Some of the traditional stations of the cross are used. It might be beneficial if these were actually reproduced on an overhead projector. The special hymn, a verse for each station, can be sung to one of a number of tunes, such as *Picardy, Rhuddlan* or *Westminster Abbey.*

This part of the service needs a short explanation beforehand – then it can proceed without announcements which is much better. Readers should be asked not to announce book, chapter or verse, but confine themselves to the title given. The tune for the hymn can be played over completely at this point, after which it should need only a chord from the organ to start it off – no announcement or playover. It really is important that this part of the service flows without interruption, or the atmosphere is lost.

At the end of the order of service is a congregational copy of *The Way of the Cross,* for photocopying on two sides.

# ORDER OF SERVICE

WELCOME AND EXPLANATION

For the main part of this service, we shall follow the way of the cross, using dialogues to help us relate that event to the present day. That will be further explained at the time.

Before that, we begin with a hymn and some prayers

HYMN        Praise to the holiest in the height
            *or* My song is love unknown

PRAYERS OF ADORATION AND CONFESSION

Here we contemplate Mystery. Here we adore perfect holiness. Let us in silence express what words cannot say

*Silence*

Let us continue in silence as we bring to the cross of Christ those things of which our consciences are afraid. Let us bring to the cross the sins of those who crucified Christ, which are our sins also – our pride, our jealousy, our complacency, our narrow-mindedness. These and more we bring to the cross.

*Silence*

ASSURANCE OF PARDON

You see, at just the right time, when we were still powerless, Christ died for the ungodly. Very rarely will anyone die for a righteous man, though for a good man someone might possibly dare to die. But God demonstrates his own love for us in this: While we were still sinners, Christ died for us. Romans 5:6-8

THE LORD'S PRAYER

READING      Mark 8:34-38

HYMN         O dearest Lord
             *or* O sacred head

## THE WAY OF THE CROSS

EXPLANATION

The next part of the service needs to flow smoothly, so a few words of explanation before we start are in order. Please refer to the orders of service. We shall follow the way of the cross, stopping at various points on the way to remember specific events, and reflect upon them. We shall be helped in this by readings and some dialogue. At the end of the dialogue there will be a response, followed by one verse of a hymn. Both the response and the hymn are on the orders of service. We shall remain seated for the hymn.

In the interests of maintaining the flow, the organist will play over the tune for the hymn now, before we begin, and from then on, there will be no playover – just a chord from the organ.

## 1  Jesus is Condemned to Death

*Reader*  Jesus is condemned to death.
Now it was the custom at the Feast to release a prisoner whom the people requested. A man called Barabbas was in prison with the insurrectionists who had committed murder in the uprising. The crowd came up and asked Pilate to do for them what he usually did. 'Do you want me to release to you the king of the Jews?' asked Pilate, knowing it was out of envy that the chief priests had handed Jesus over to him. But the chief priests stirred up the crowd to have Pilate release Barabbas instead. 'What shall I do, then, with the one you call the king of the Jews?' Pilate asked them. 'Crucify him!' they shouted. 'Why? What crime has he committed?' asked Pilate. But they shouted all the louder, 'Crucify him!' Wanting to satisfy the crowd, Pilate released Barabbas to them. He had Jesus flogged, and handed him over to be crucified[1].

*Voice 1*  Not a question of justice,

*Voice 2*  more a question of keeping the punters happy.

*Voice 1*  Pilate knows Jesus is innocent,

*Voice 2*  but he cares more for a quiet life than for justice.

*Voice 1*  So a murderer goes free

*Voice 2*  and an innocent man dies in his place.

*Voice 1*  You'd think an event like this would wake us up to injustice,

*Voice 2*  but it doesn't.

*Voice 1*  Still today, self-righteous public opinion cries out for blood.

*Voice 2*  It doesn't matter who pays,

*Voice 1*  as long as someone does.

*Voice 2*  So the innocent suffer

*Voice 1*  in place of the guilty.

*Voice 2*  The rabble is pacified.

*Voice 1*  And the privileged sleep soundly in their beds.

*Minister*  Let us follow Jesus.

*All*  Let us walk the way of the cross.

---

[1] Mark 15:6-15

HYMN
Jesus, universal Victim,
keep us ever at your side,
when the brutal are protected
and the gentle crucified.
Fill us with your suff'ring Spirit,
so to turn oppression's tide.

## 2  THE CROSS IS LAID UPON JESUS

Reader
The cross is laid upon Jesus.
He was despised and rejected by others; a man of suffering and acquainted with infirmity; and as one from whom others hide their faces he was despised, and we held him of no account. Surely he has borne our infirmities and carried our diseases; yet we accounted him stricken, struck down by God, and afflicted. But he was wounded for our transgressions, crushed for our iniquities; upon him was the punishment that made us whole, and by his bruises we are healed[2].

Voice 1
The weight of the cross that Jesus bore was much more than just the wood from which it was made.

Voice 2
It included a terrible burden of fear.

Voice 1
The fears of the privileged

Voice 2
afraid of losing their positions

Voice 1
The fears of the narrow-minded

Voice 2
afraid of losing their prejudices.

Voice 1
And still, today, when the powerful are threatened,

Voice 2
it's the innocent who get punished.

Voice 1
It's the weak who carry the load.

Voice 2
History repeats itself.

Voice 1
Has to.

Voice 2
Nobody listens.

Minister
Let us follow Jesus.

All
Let us walk the way of the cross.

HYMN
Son of man, the burden bearing
of a world of sin and fear;
grant us, in our greed and anger,
eyes to see and ears to hear,
where the poor and humble suffer,
grace and judgement ever near.

[2] Isaiah 53:3-5

### 3 JESUS FALLS

| | |
|---|---|
| *Reader* | Jesus falls.<br>Let the same mind be in you that was in Christ Jesus who, though he was in the form of God, did not regard equality with God as something to be exploited, but emptied himself, taking the form of a slave, being born in human likeness. And being found in human form, he humbled himself and became obedient to the point of death – even death on a cross.[3] |
| *Voice 1* | God in the dust. |
| *Voice 2* | Not a pretty sight; |
| *Voice 1* | not particularly god-like, either. |
| *Voice 2* | But that's the kind of God he is, |
| *Voice 1* | the kind of God he chooses to be: |
| *Voice 2* | cares about his people |
| *Voice 1* | more than his own dignity. |
| *Voice 2* | And as long as there are people there, |
| *Voice 1* | in the dust, |
| *Voice 2* | burdened by oppression, |
| *Voice 1* | crushed by greed, |
| *Voice 2* | carrying the troubles of the world on their backs; |
| *Voice 1* | as long as they are in the dust, |
| *Voice 2* | God will be there too. |
| *Voice 1* | That's the kind of God he is. |
| *Voice 2* | That's the kind of God he chooses to be. |
| *Minister* | Let us follow Jesus. |
| *All* | Let us walk the way of the cross. |
| | |
| HYMN | Lord of all, renouncing glory<br>in complete humility;<br>from the bonds of pride and status<br>set your captive people free,<br>by your sorrow redefining<br>human worth and dignity |

[3] Philippians 2:5-8

## 4  THE CROSS IS LAID UPON SIMON OF CYRENE

Reader     The cross is laid upon Simon of Cyrene.
           A certain man from Cyrene, Simon, the father of Alexander and Rufus, was passing by on his way in from the country, and they forced him to carry the cross.[4]

Voice 1    Just a passer-by;

Voice 2    what did it have to do with him?

Voice 1    He was only a visitor,

Voice 2    who happened to be in the wrong place at the wrong time,

Voice 1    but all that burden was laid upon him.

Voice 2    That's the way it is with injustice.

Voice 1    It's no respecter of persons.

Voice 2    Jesus was the victim,

Voice 1    but other people got drawn into it.

Voice 2    Still, at least it meant that Jesus was not alone.

Voice 1    Bad enough to get crucified,

Voice 2    without having to carry your own cross.

Voice 1    Perhaps that's our role.

Voice 2    The poor get crucified;

Voice 1    we can't always stop it happening,

Voice 2    but that doesn't mean we can't get involved at all.

Minister   Let us follow Jesus.

All        Let us walk the way of the cross.

HYMN       Still the broken victim stumbles
           up the steep and rocky road,
           bent beneath the heavy burden
           our injustice has bestowed.
           Where the weight of sin oppresses,
           give us grace to bear the load

## 5  THE WOMEN OF JERUSALEM WEEP FOR JESUS

Reader     The women of Jerusalem weep for Jesus.
           A large number of people followed him, including women who mourned and wailed for him. Jesus turned and said to them, 'Daughters of Jerusalem, do not weep for me; weep for yourselves and for your children. For the time will come when you will say,

---

[4] Mark 15:21

"Blessed are the barren women, the wombs that never bore and the breasts that never nursed!" Then they will say to the mountains, "Fall on us!" and to the hills, "Cover us!" For if men do these things when the tree is green, what will happen when it is dry?"[5]

| | |
|---|---|
| *Voice 1* | Women and children first: |
| *Voice 2* | first to feel the effects of poverty; |
| *Voice 1* | first to suffer under injustice. |
| *Voice 2* | Perhaps it's because they're more vulnerable, |
| *Voice 1* | or perhaps they have more to lose, |
| *Voice 2* | but where there's injustice, all around the world, |
| *Voice 1* | there you'll find women. |
| *Voice 2* | Watching. |
| *Voice 1* | Weeping. |
| *Voice 2* | Waiting. |
| *Voice 1* | Praying. |
| *Voice 2* | Staying faithful |
| *Voice 1* | even when there's no point any more, |
| *Voice 2* | because, even when everything else is pointless, |
| *Voice 1* | there's always a point in loyalty; |
| *Voice 2* | there's always a point in faithfulness; |
| *Voice 1* | there's always a point in prayer. |
| *Minister* | Let us follow Jesus. |
| *All* | Let us walk the way of the cross. |

*Hymn*  Women stand in sorrow weeping,
where the Saviour treads his way,
crying still in pain and anger
for the victims of today
Women stay, though others scatter,
risking all to watch and pray!

### 6  Jesus is Stripped of his Garments

*Reader*  Jesus is stripped of his garments.
They came to a place called Golgotha (which means The Place of the Skull). There they offered Jesus wine to drink, mixed with gall; but after tasting it, he refused to drink it. When they had crucified him, they divided up his clothes by casting lots. And sitting down, they kept watch over him there.[6]

[5] Luke 23:27-31  [6] Matt 27:33-36

| | |
|---|---|
| *Voice 1* | The garments are removed. |
| *Voice 2* | The body is revealed: |
| *Voice 1* | a most unattractive body, |
| *Voice 2* | bruised by the beatings, |
| *Voice 1* | lacerated by the scourging, |
| *Voice 2* | humiliated by public exposure, |
| *Voice 1* | the body of Christ. |
| *Voice 2* | That is what the church is called. |
| *Voice 1* | Strip off its garments; |
| *Voice 2* | remove the trappings of wealth and dignity: |
| *Voice 1* | what kind of body would we find? |
| *Voice 2* | Smooth, unblemished, untouched by the evil of the world? |
| *Voice 1* | Or marked and disfigured? |
| *Voice 2* | A sign of complacency? |
| *Voice 1* | Or a sign of hope? |
| *Minister* | Let us follow Jesus. |
| *All* | Let us walk the way of the cross. |

| | |
|---|---|
| HYMN | Church of God, arrayed in splendour, |
| | risen body of the Lord: |
| | shed the garb of worldly glory; |
| | show the marks of nail and sword. |
| | Where the poor and humble suffer, |
| | be of hope the sign and word. |

### 7  JESUS IS NAILED TO THE CROSS

| | |
|---|---|
| *Reader* | Jesus is nailed to the cross. |
| | They crucified Jesus, and with him two others – one on each side and Jesus in the middle. Pilate had a notice prepared and fastened to the cross. It read: JESUS OF NAZARETH, THE KING OF THE JEWS. Many of the Jews read this sign, for the place where Jesus was crucified was near the city, and the sign was written in Aramaic, Latin and Greek. The chief priests of the Jews protested to Pilate, 'Do not write 'The King of the Jews', but that this man claimed to be king of the Jews.' Pilate answered, 'What I have written, I have written.'[7] |
| *Voice 1* | So this is the king! |
| *Voice 2* | Very different from the traditional ideas; |
| *Voice 1* | very different from most present-day ideas. |

[7] John 19:18-22

| | |
|---|---|
| *Voice 2* | The world is ruled by a crucified man, |
| *Voice 1* | not by the one who does the crucifying. |
| *Voice 2* | The world is ruled by love, |
| *Voice 1* | not by tyranny. |
| *Voice 2* | The world is ruled by forgiveness, |
| *Voice 1* | not by vengeance. |
| *Voice 2* | The world is ruled by faith, |
| *Voice 1* | not by fear. |
| *Voice 2* | So all our ideas about power, |
| *Voice 1* | all our ideas about wisdom, |
| *Voice 2* | are exposed as the weakness and folly they are, |
| *Voice 1* | by a carpenter nailed to a tree. |
| *Minister* | Let us follow Jesus. |
| *All* | Let us walk the way of the cross. |

HYMN      All the pow'rs of darkness gather
          where the hammer meets the nail,
          and, confronted with compassion,
          malice and coercion fail.
          Love outweighs the power of evil,
          on the universal scale.

PRAYERS OF INTERCESSION

> *The prayers are mainly silent. In each section, following again the
> 'Way of the Cross', an opening bidding is followed by silence,
> which ends with the response:*
>
>> *Lord, hear us.*
>> **Lord, graciously hear us.**

We pray with Jesus, as he is condemned, for all who are
unjustly condemned, because of the baying of the crowds.

*Silence*

Lord, hear us.
**Lord, graciously hear us.**

We pray with Jesus, as he takes up his cross, for all who bear the burden of
the fears and resentments of others.

*Silence*

Lord, hear us.
**Lord, graciously hear us.**

We pray with Jesus as he falls, for all who fall under the weight of oppression,
that they may recognise God among them.

*Silence*

Lord, hear us.
**Lord, graciously hear us.**

We pray with Simon of Cyrene, for all who walk with the victims of injustice, and share their load, and we give thanks for them.

*Silence*

Lord, hear us.
**Lord, graciously hear us.**

We pray with the women of Jerusalem for all who watch,
and wait, and weep, longing for justice

*Silence*

Lord, hear us.
**Lord, graciously hear us.**

We pray with Jesus, as he is stripped of his garments,
for grace to be his broken body in the world

*Silence*

Lord, hear us.
**Lord, graciously hear us.**

We pray with Jesus, as he is nailed to the cross, for all who struggle to confront injustice with love, and despair with hope.

*Silence*

Lord, hear us.
**Lord, graciously hear us.**

HYMN          When I survey the wondrous cross

BENEDICTION

There follows a congregational copy of the service, for photocopying on 2 sides.

## The Way of the Cross

### 1 JESUS IS CONDEMNED TO DEATH

Reading
Dialogue
*Minister*  Let us follow Jesus.
*All*  **Let us walk the way of the cross.**

Hymn  Jesus, universal Victim,
keep us ever at your side,
when the brutal are protected
and the gentle crucified.
Fill us with your suff'ring Spirit,
so to turn oppression's tide.

### 2 THE CROSS IS LAID UPON JESUS

Reading
Dialogue
*Minister*  Let us follow Jesus.
*All*  **Let us walk the way of the cross.**

Hymn  Son of man, the burden bearing
of a world of sin and fear;
grant us, in our greed and anger,
eyes to see and ears to hear,
where the poor and humble suffer,
grace and judgement ever near.

### 3 JESUS FALLS

Reading
Dialogue
*Minister*  Let us follow Jesus.
*All*  **Let us walk the way of the cross.**

Hymn  Lord of all, renouncing glory
in complete humility;
from the bonds of pride and status
set your captive people free,
by your sorrow redefining
human worth and dignity.

### 4 THE CROSS IS LAID UPON SIMON OF CYRENE

Reading
Dialogue
*Minister*  Let us follow Jesus.
*All*  **Let us walk the way of the cross.**

| | |
|---|---|
| Hymn | Still the broken victim stumbles |
| | up the steep and rocky road, |
| | bent beneath the heavy burden |
| | our injustice has bestowed. |
| | Where the weight of sin oppresses, |
| | give us grace to bear the load. |

## 5 THE WOMEN OF JERUSALEM WEEP FOR JESUS

| | |
|---|---|
| Reading | |
| Dialogue | |
| *Minister* | Let us follow Jesus. |
| *All* | **Let us walk the way of the cross.** |

| | |
|---|---|
| Hymn | Women stand in sorrow weeping, |
| | where the Saviour treads his way, |
| | crying still in pain and anger |
| | for the victims of today. |
| | Women stay, though others scatter, |
| | risking all to watch and pray! |

## 6 JESUS IS STRIPPED OF HIS GARMENTS

| | |
|---|---|
| Reading | |
| Dialogue | |
| *Minister* | Let us follow Jesus. |
| *All* | **Let us walk the way of the cross.** |

| | |
|---|---|
| Hymn | Church of God, arrayed in splendour, |
| | risen body of the Lord: |
| | shed the garb of worldly glory; |
| | show the marks of nail and sword. |
| | Where the poor and humble suffer, |
| | be of hope the sign and word. |

## 7 JESUS IS NAILED TO THE CROSS

| | |
|---|---|
| Reading | |
| Dialogue | |
| *Minister* | Let us follow Jesus. |
| *All* | **Let us walk the way of the cross.** |

| | |
|---|---|
| Hymn | All the pow'rs of darkness gather |
| | where the hammer meets the nail, |
| | and, confronted with compassion, |
| | malice and coercion fail. |
| | Love outweighs the power of evil, |
| | on the universal scale. |

From *Fasts and Festivals* by Michael Forster, © Kevin Mayhew Ltd., Rattlesden, Bury St. Edmunds, Suffolk, IP30 0SZ

# EASTER SERVICE

IN WORD and sacrament, we celebrate new life (as distinct from an extra helping of the old)! And we celebrate it not only as past event and future hope, but as present reality. The risen Christ meets us in the present, reminds us of the past, and leads us forward. We share the communion as a sign of all three, and as a sign of our willingness to accept the new life Christ offers, with all its implications and responsibilities.

# ORDER OF SERVICE

*As the congregation arrive, they are given tapers, or small hand-held candles (the latter must include drip trays or holders). These will be used at the end of the service, when the light of Easter is spread through the congregation.*

OPENING PROCLAMATION

| | |
|---|---|
| *Minister* | Christ is risen! |
| *All* | He is risen indeed! |

| | |
|---|---|
| HYMN | Jesus lives, thy terrors now |
| | *or* Majesty |

PRAYERS OF ADORATION AND CONFESSION

Eternal God, it is with joy and wonder that we come to celebrate resurrection. In a very special sense, this is indeed the day that you have made. Your power, made perfect in weakness, has brought joy out of the very heart of pain. We recognise here, not the power of brute strength, but that of suffering love. You have shown us in the cross that the only power you want to use is the power of persuasion, moving our hearts to repentance and faith by your constant presence in the midst of indifference and rejection. The life which we celebrate today has been won at that cost, and we have no words to express the love you inspire in us. So accept the silent wonder of our hearts.

*Silence*

Holy God, despite the assurance of Easter, we still fail to trust your love as we should. We still long for security, for certainty, and we still embrace the power images of the world, rather than that of Calvary. Forgive us our lack of faith, and call us again to live in life-renewing hope, through Jesus Christ our Lord. Amen

ASSURANCE OF PARDON

But now, this is what the Lord says – he who created you, O Jacob, he who formed you, O Israel: 'Fear not, for I have redeemed you; I have summoned you by name; you are mine. When you pass through the waters, I will be with you; and when you pass through the rivers, they will not sweep over you. When you walk through the fire, you will not be burned; the flames will not set you ablaze . . . you are precious and honoured in my sight, and . . . I love you.'

*Isaiah 43:1,2,4*

THE LORD'S PRAYER

| | |
|---|---|
| HYMN | Jesus Christ is risen today |
| | *or* The day of resurrection |

## THE CELEBRATION OF THE WORD

READING       Exodus 14:15-22

DIALOGUE IN A PRISON CELL

| | |
|---|---|
| *Voice 1* | Aren't you due to be released today? |
| *Voice 2* | (*gloomily*) Oh, that's right – rub it in, why don't you! |
| *Voice 1* | Aren't you happy about it? |
| *Voice 2* | Well, I know I should be, but I'm nervous. |
| *Voice 1* | What about? |
| *Voice 2* | Look, I know this place is no great shakes, but I'm beginning to think it's got its good points. |
| *Voice 1* | As far as I'm concerned, the only good point is that you get out eventually – and you are! |
| *Voice 2* | Oh, I don't like it here. But on the other hand, at least I know where I stand. |
| *Voice 1* | What d'you mean? |
| *Voice 2* | Well, there's a routine – life has some order about it. |
| *Voice 1* | Of course it has: 'Do this', 'Don't do that' . . . |
| *Voice 2* | You can mock, but in here I've got my bed and board. |
| *Voice 1* | Are you actually saying you want to stay here? |
| *Voice 2* | Not really, I hate the place. But at least it's something I know. It'd be different for you – you've got a family. I've got no-one out there. No-one and nothing. |
| *Voice 1* | So, it's a great adventure – get out there and enjoy it! |
| *Voice 2* | If I knew what was ahead of me I might – but it's the great unknown. |
| *Voice 1* | Well, you're not the first person to have to face that, and I can understand that this place has a feeling of security about it! And talking of security . . . 'morning, officer. |
| *Voice 3* | What was that I heard you saying about not wanting to go? If you really want to stay, it might be arranged. There's the toilets to be cleaned, the gutters to be unblocked, the boilers to be stoked, plenty of potatoes to be peeled . . . |
| *Voice 2* | All right, you've made your point – which way to the main gate? |

| | |
|---|---|
| HYMN | One more step along the world I go *or* Come ye faithful, raise the strain |
| READING | John 20:1-18 |

DIALOGUE

| | |
|---|---|
| *Jesus* | Don't hold on to me. |
| *Mary* | Why not? |
| *Jesus* | Because we've got to move on. |
| *Mary* | Why? |
| *Jesus* | Well, let me ask you the question:<br>why do you want to stay in this place? |
| *Mary* | It's a very beautiful place. And you're here. |
| *Jesus* | Do you think I won't be with you anywhere else? |
| *Mary* | Of course I don't, but it's nice here. |
| *Jesus* | For you and me, but what about everyone else? |
| *Mary* | That's all right – I'll go and get the disciples – you wait here for me. |
| *Jesus* | Then what will we do? |
| *Mary* | Well, you know – all the things we used to love.<br>Sing the old songs, tell the old stories . . . |
| *Jesus* | I see . . . would you like me to get some rocking chairs,<br>and some rugs to go over our knees? |
| *Mary* | That sounds nice – how clever of you to . . .<br>Why do I get the idea you're winding me up? |
| *Jesus* | Probably because I am! But really, Mary, is that what<br>you call life? We don't want to get locked into the past.<br>I'm offering you new life, which means looking forward. |
| *Mary* | So the past is irrelevant? |
| *Jesus* | No, because the future grows out of it. You must never forget<br>or reject the past, but you mustn't get locked into it, either.<br>The authorities tried to pin me down – literally – and they failed.<br>Don't you start! |
| *Mary* | So, what next? |
| *Jesus* | Go and find the disciples and – |
| *Mary* | and bring them here! That's what I was going to do in the<br>first place. |
| *Jesus* | No, you wanted to bring them back to the past. I'm asking you<br>to go and tell them that I'm leading them forward. |
| *Mary* | Where to? |
| *Jesus* | To the future! To life! To God!<br>Mary . . . |
| *Mary* | Yes, Jesus? |
| *Jesus* | Just do it! |
| *Mary* | Yes, Jesus. |

SONG        Do Not Touch *(See Appendix)*

PRAYERS OF INTERCESSION

We give thanks for life and freedom, and we pray for all who are less free, less fully alive, than they might be.

We pray for prisoners of conscience; people of any religion, or of none, who are persecuted for their faith. (especially . . .)

*Silence*

God of all creation,
**fill the world with life.**

We pray for the poor; for all who are denied fullness of life by the greed of others. (especially . . .)

*Silence*

God of all creation,
**fill the world with life.**

We pray for the greedy, all who seek to monopolise life and freedom, that they might find real life by taking the risk of loving others. (especially . . .)

*Silence*

God of all creation,
**fill the world with life.**

We pray for people affected by war, deprived of homes, dignity, future. (especially . . .)

*Silence*

God of all creation,
**fill the world with life.**

We pray for all whose lives are stunted because of prejudices,
either their own or other people's. (especially . . .)

*Silence*

God of all creation,
**fill the world with life.**

We pray for the church – that we may be a sign of life in the world. (especially . . .)

*Silence*

God of all creation,
**fill the world with life.**

We pray for all who are denied the fullness of life, because of sickness, infirmity or anxiety. (especially . . .)

*Silence*

God of all creation,
**fill the world with life.**

We pray for the bereaved, for those near to death and for those who care for them. (especially . . .)

*Silence*

God of all creation,
**fill the world with life.**

We pray for ourselves, knowing that we are less free, less fully alive, than we are created to be. Holy God, we pray that we might be healed of the fears and prejudices which entomb us, and set free in the world as a sign of life and hope, through Jesus Christ our Lord. Amen

## THE CELEBRATION OF THE SACRAMENT

### THE PEACE

Jesus taught us, before offering our gifts, to be at peace with one another:

The peace of God be with you all.
**And also with you.**

### OFFERTORY

### INVITATION

On this of all days, we remember that we are here at the invitation, and in the presence, of the risen Christ. It is his celebration, and it is from him that the invitation goes out. Come, then, in penitence and faith, in adoration and wonder; most of all, come in the assurance that Christ died for all, and all have a place at his table. But we must not come unprepared. So let us be silent, and open ourselves to his presence.

*Silence*

### PRAYER OF THANKSGIVING

Eternal God and Father, we offer you our praise and thanksgiving:
for the creation of your world in all its richness and glory;
for your gracious work of redemption in liberating the oppressed,
renewing the weary and forgiving the sinful;
for your calling of men and women to share in the work of salvation
in the story of Israel and our story;
for Jesus Christ our Lord, the eternal Word made flesh,
sharing our humanity and revealing your love and compassion;
for his life and ministry in word and action,
his lifting up of the lowly and his healing of the broken;
for his redeeming death on the cross for all humanity,
of which this bread and this cup are the symbol and sign.

We thank you for raising him to life again and exalting him
so that we might call him 'Lord', as we offer him our allegiance
and seek to share his way.

We thank you for the gift of your Holy Spirit, powerfully present in your people and your world, for the fellowship of your church, for all the means of grace and the hope of glory.

Living God, fill us with your Spirit, that as we share this bread and this wine we may feed on the body and blood of Christ, and be empowered for service in your world.

Accept our prayers and thanksgiving in the name of Jesus Christ, the light of the world and the life of your people.

From *Patterns and Prayers for Christian Worship* © 1991 Baptist Union

WORDS OF INSTITUTION
*During these words, the bread is broken and the cup elevated,*
*in full view of the congregation*

For I received from the Lord what I also passed on to you: The Lord Jesus, on the night he was betrayed, took bread, and when he had given thanks, he broke it and said, 'This is my body, which is for you; do this in remembrance of me.' In the same way, after supper he took the cup, saying, 'This cup is the new covenant in my blood; do this, whenever you drink it, in remembrance of me.' For whenever you eat this bread and drink this cup, you proclaim the Lord's death until he comes.        *1 Corinthians 11:23-26*

*A brief silence*

SHARING OF BREAD AND WINE

POST-COMMUNION PRAYER
Holy God, we thank you for welcoming us to this table, to celebrate the resurrection of Christ from the dead. Send us out in the world, in power of your Spirit, to live his risen life and to be, by grace, a sign of life, through him, Jesus Christ our Lord, Amen.

SPREADING THE LIGHT
*Some children light tapers from the Easter Candle and, from them, light the congregation's tapers. (It is best to invite the congregation to find the next hymn first, while they still have both hands free.)*

HYMN        From the very depths of darkness *(See Appendix)*
*or* Christ is risen!

BLESSING
Now go from here, in the power of the risen Christ, to be signs of his life wherever death seems rampant. And the blessing of God, Father, Son and Holy Spirit, be with you all, evermore.
**Amen.**

# CHURCH ANNIVERSARY SERVICE

MANY CHURCHES, especially in the Free Church traditions, have an annual Anniversary Service, commemorating the foundation of that particular congregation. This can be especially useful at this time when the teaching of Christianity in schools can no longer be taken for granted (rightly or wrongly) and we cannot assume that the basic stories and images of the faith are known. Churches are being called upon to accept the responsibility for that. The service included here explores one aspect of faith, as a journey of liberation and discovery.

When this service was first prepared, a lot of children were expected to be present, and then the minister carelessly mislaid his voice the day before the service. So the service had to be quickly adapted so that it could be led by others with absolutely minimal preparation, and involve the children in meaningful ways. What follows is the result.

An Annual Covenant Service is also becoming increasingly popular in churches, as an occasion to renew commitment. We decided to hold one immediately following the Anniversary Service.

Like the Jewish Passover, but on a much smaller scale, this meal fulfils a number of functions.

It is an anniversary celebration – celebrating the freedom to which Christ has led us. It is also a covenant meal, renewing our commitment to each other as a covenant community. And it is a learning opportunity – a chance to hear again some of the basic ideas and themes of the faith.

As the meal progresses, scripted dialogues take place, picking up ideas initially presented in the service, and of course the great covenant meal of the Christian tradition – the Communion – is incorporated into the meal. This is done, in biblical fashion, the bread being blessed, broken and shared before the main food is served, and the cup taken 'likewise, after supper . . .'

This works best if people remain seated throughout, at the meal table, and the elements are served to them there. This practice will be familiar to many Free-Church worshippers, but will need some careful planning where it is less usual.

The menu depends upon resources and personnel. It can be a very simple meal – perhaps soup, followed by a filled jacket potato, with fruit as a sweet – or something very elaborate. We found, by experience, that the dialogues were best read between courses, rather than during them, but again it is a matter of what works best in each particular setting.

# ORDER OF SERVICE

**WELCOME**

Welcome to our Anniversary Service. A special welcome if you are a visitor, or a newcomer to this church. The idea today is to explore one of the basic ideas of Christianity, which is that of a journey. We talk about 'following' Jesus, which itself seems to suggest a journey, and of course the Old Testament people were continually being called on journeys – Abraham and Moses are two particularly popular examples, but there are many others. Christians are not people who know it all, but are constantly learning. We are not the ones who have 'arrived', but life is one long journey of adventure and discovery, following where God leads us.

We're going to be looking at that idea in more detail, as we go through the service. Now, we shall sing the first hymn.

**HYMN**      Come, let us join our cheerful songs
            *or* Come on and celebrate

**PRAYER OF APPROACH**

Eternal God, we are here to learn and to celebrate. We remember your faithfulness to your people through the ages, and in particular to those who have worshipped in this place before us. You have called us to share freely in your love, and to proclaim it to the world. As we celebrate your story, let us be aware of your presence here, calling us forward to renewal of faith, of hope and of love, leading us toward greater freedom. In a world often fickle and unreliable, you are the one in whom we can trust, and for that we give you heartfelt praise, through Jesus Christ our Lord,
**Amen.**

**PRAYER OF CONFESSION**

Holy God, forgive us for our lack of trust. Forgive us for the smallness of our vision, when we see only the difficulties ahead and not the hope. Forgive us for trying to follow you on our terms, for carrying with us the burdens of prejudice, fear, possessions and selfishness which we call 'security'. Forgive us, and help us truly to open ourselves to your love and respond to your call, through Jesus Christ our Lord,
**Amen.**

**ASSURANCE OF PARDON**

If we claim to be without sin, we deceive ourselves and the truth is not in us. If we confess our sins, [God] is faithful and just and will forgive us our sins and purify us from all unrighteousness.                                    *1 John 1:8-9*

**READING**      Exodus 2:1-10

FIRST DIALOGUE

| | |
|---|---|
| *Voice 1* | D'you remember what happened to that baby? |
| *Voice 2* | Didn't he grow up to be a great leader? |
| *Voice 1* | Yes, he was the person God used to lead the people of Israel to freedom. |
| *Voice 2* | That's very exciting, isn't it? |
| *Voice 1* | Why do you particularly say that? |
| *Voice 2* | Because that means that it was from right in the middle of the despair that the hope came. |
| *Voice 1* | I see what you mean – not some outsider, |
| *Voice 2* | like Superman, |
| *Voice 1* | or the US Cavalry, |
| *Voice 2* | riding to the rescue at the last minute. |
| *Voice 1* | No – from right in the middle of the situation, in all the despair, |
| *Voice 2* | hope begins in a very tiny way, |
| *Voice 1* | as a little baby, hidden away from the authorities. |
| *Voice 2* | Then he grew up, and God called him . . . |
| *Voice 1* | speaking from the middle of a burning bush, wasn't it? |
| *Voice 2* | Yes – amazing – the bush was full of fire, but wasn't burnt by it – so Moses knew it must be something special. |
| *Voice 1* | And that's where God told him he had to lead the people out of slavery to freedom. |
| *Voice 2* | Moses wasn't very happy about it. |
| *Voice 1* | He didn' t think he was up to the job . . . |
| *Voice 2* | did his best to fail the interview! |
| *Voice 1* | But God had decided he was the one. |
| *Voice 2* | And it did not matter how feeble Moses was, |
| *Voice 1* | because God helped him. |

HYMN    Moses I know you're the man
*or* One more step along the world I go

READING    Luke 2: 1-7

SECOND DIALOGUE

| | |
|---|---|
| *Voice 1* | There it is again! |
| *Voice 2* | There what is again? |
| *Voice 1* | The same idea – a little baby, in a dangerous place, where people are frightened. |

| | |
|---|---|
| *Voice 2* | who grew up to lead people to freedom. |
| *Voice 1* | But this was a bit different – he recognised that a lot of the things that make people slaves are actually inside them: |
| *Voice 2* | things like fear, |
| *Voice 1* | worrying what the neighbours will say, |
| *Voice 2* | worrying about the future . . . |
| *Voice 1* | Some people run their whole lives on the basis of what they're afraid of. |
| *Voice 2* | Jesus came to free people from all that. |
| *Voice 1* | He showed that it's better to live on the basis of trust, |
| *Voice 2* | and love, |
| *Voice 1* | and caring for one another. |
| *Voice 2* | But people don't often change instantly, do they? |
| *Voice 1* | It's a bit like what Moses did – leading people on a journey. |
| *Voice 2* | From the kind of people they are now . . . |
| *Voice 1* | to the kind of people God can help them to be. |
| *Voice 2* | But they need a leader. |
| *Voice 1* | That's why God always sends one – he did with Moses, and he did with Jesus. |
| *Voice 2* | I wonder if any of these people would like to go on a journey. |
| *Voice 1* | Let's find out. Let's play 'follow-my-leader' around the church. |
| *Voice 2* | And don't forget to do whatever the leader does. |

*The children follow around the church, imitating whatever the leader does as they go. If some adults can be induced to join in, so much the better!*

| | |
|---|---|
| HYMN | Lord Jesus Christ (omitting optional communion verse) *or* We are people on a journey *(See Appendix)* |

THIRD DIALOGUE

| | |
|---|---|
| *Voice 1* | Of course, it's easy to trust when you know where you're going. |
| *Voice 2* | But Jesus calls for a little more than that – he calls us to trust when we don't know. |
| *Voice 1* | That's a bit like being a Rainbow – or a guide, or a scout, or whatever –[1] |
| *Voice 2* | It's also like being a member of a church . . . |
| *Voice 1* | . . . or a club . . . |

[1]Use the names of whatever organisations the church has. If none, the dialogue will need slight adaptation.

Voice 2    . . . or anything at all – I wonder how many of these children have done things they never expected to do.

Voice 1    Possibly, things they never even thought they'd be able to do.

*(It might be appropriate to break off the dialogue and explore that idea with the children. Otherwise, simply continue)*

Voice 2    I expect there were a lot of fears to overcome:

Voice 1    fear of looking silly,

Voice 2    fear of getting hurt,

Voice 1    and life is a lot more fun when those fears have been overcome.

Voice 2    But they wouldn't do any of that if they didn't trust the leader.

Voice 1    That's how it is for Christians – life's a lot better if we can be set free from our fears

Voice 2    But before that can happen, we have to trust the leader.

HYMN    The Journey of life
        *or* Lead us, heavenly Father, lead us

PRAYERS OF INTERCESSION

We offer prayers for the world and, in particular, for people who are enslaved by ideas – who oppress or terrorise others in the name of one political ideology or another – and for those who are oppressed by them.

*(In particular we pray for:)*

God of Moses, and Father of Jesus:
**lead the slaves to freedom.**

We pray for those in the developing world, who are enslaved by international markets; who work long hours for unjust wages, producing cheap luxuries for the prosperous to enjoy.

*(In particular we pray for:)*

God of Moses, and Father of Jesus:
**lead the slaves to freedom.**

We pray for all who are enslaved by wealth, possessions and the desire for security, and who thereby contribute to the enslavement of others.

*(In particular we pray for:)*

God of Moses, and Father of Jesus:
**lead the slaves to freedom.**

We pray for all who are enslaved by religious dogma, and are unwilling or are discouraged from making faith's journey of discovery.

*(In particular, we pray for:)*

God of Moses, and Father of Jesus:
**lead the slaves to freedom.**

We pray for all whose lives are impoverished by fear, sickness, and anxiety.

*(In particular, we pray for:)*

Finally, as we join our worship with the whole communion of saints, we pray for the bereaved.

*(In particular, we pray for:)*

We give thanks for those we love whom we can no longer see, grateful for all they have allowed us to share with them, and we commend them and ourselves into the unfailing care of God, through Jesus Christ our Lord, **Amen.**

OFFERING

HYMN          Lord of the Dance
                      *or* You shall go out with joy

BENEDICTION

May God himself, who brought the people of Israel out of Egypt, and raised Jesus from the dead, free you from the chains of this present world, and lead you into the glorious mystery of eternal salvation. And the blessing of God, Father, Son and Holy Spirit, be with you all, evermore.
**Amen.**

# ANNIVERSARY COMMUNION MEAL

### WELCOME AND EXPLANATION

Welcome to this Covenant Meal. We shall follow the biblical pattern for communion: the bread will be blessed and broken before the meal starts and then, after the meal, we shall take the cup. The idea of this meal is that, like the Passover, it should fulfil a number of functions.

It is an anniversary celebration – celebrating the freedom to which Christ has led us. It is also a covenant meal, renewing our commitment to each other as a covenant community. And it is a learning opportunity – a chance to hear again some of the basic ideas and themes of the faith. We have begun that during worship, with the readings we had then, and during this meal we shall be helped to reflect upon that by some conversations which will take place as we eat. But please do not feel you have to go through the whole meal in silence – relax, converse, and generally enjoy the fellowship of the meal. Occasionally, you will be called to silence so that something else can happen but, apart from that, please relax and enjoy yourselves.

First, let us hear the Gospel

### GOSPEL     John 15:12-17

### PRAYER OF THANKSGIVING

Holy God, we give you thanks for your covenant, established long ago with your people, constantly renewed in love and forgiveness, and finally sealed in the life, death and resurrection of your Son Jesus Christ. We thank you for his life of love and obedience, lived in constant fellowship with you by the power of the Holy Spirit. We thank you that by his life, death and resurrection, he opened the way to life eternal, inviting all creation to share in his perfect fellowship with you, in the Holy Spirit. We pray that by the power of that same Spirit we may receive this bread and wine as the body and blood of Christ, and be united in sacrificial service to the world. As the bread is broken and the wine poured out, so may we offer our lives to be broken and poured in his service, for the wholeness of creation.

We give you thanks for the communion of saints, with whom, by your grace, we share this holy covenant. So we join with the church throughout the world, and with the whole company of heaven in offering you praise and thanksgiving. Accept this sacrifice of praise, and the continuing sacrifice of our daily lives, through Jesus Christ our Lord, Amen.

### WORDS OF INSTITUTION (1) (INCLUDING THE BREAKING OF THE BREAD)

For I received from the Lord what I also passed on to you: The Lord Jesus, on the night he was betrayed, took bread, and when he had given thanks, he broke it and said, 'This is my body, which is for you; do this in remembrance of me.'
*1 Corinthians 11:23-24*

THE SHARING OF THE BREAD

*The bread is distributed to the people, as they sit at the meal table.*

PRAYER

We thank you, holy God, for calling us to participate in your covenant. Strengthen our commitment as we share this meal, and send us out to be the body of Christ in the world. Amen.

SOUP OR STARTER (IF PROVIDED)

FIRST DIALOGUE

| | |
|---|---|
| *Voice 1* | What I don' t understand is, why did God have to bother with Moses? If he wanted his people to be free, why didn't he just snap his fingers and make it happen? |
| *Voice 2* | Because that would not have been taking them seriously. They had to follow because they wanted to – not because they hadn't got any choice. |
| *Voice 1* | O K, but that still doesn't explain all that forty years in the wilderness stuff. Why was that necessary? |
| *Voice 2* | Becoming a free people meant a lot more than just being removed from slavery. There was a lot of learning to be done before they could be really free. They'd never had to think for themselves, or take responsibility for themselves before. |
| *Voice 1* | So it was a chance to grow up? |
| *Voice 2* | Yes – in all kinds of ways. They had to learn about God and his purposes; they had to learn to take a longer-term view of things. Perhaps most difficult of all, they had to learn to be a community – to get on together. |
| *Voice 1* | And that's what took them forty years to do? |
| *Voice 2* | That's right. It has been said that it took God no time at all to get Israel out of Egypt. The problem was getting Egypt out of Israel – getting rid of all the memories, and anxieties, and hang-ups that slavery had caused. |
| *Voice 1* | So that's what faith is about – a journey towards freedom |
| *Voice 2* | And it's a journey we make together – as a covenant community. |
| *Voice 1* | A bit risky, though, wasn't it – all that stuff about crossing the Red Sea? I don't think I'd fancy walking across a sea-bed with twenty feet of water piled up on each side of me. |
| *Voice 2* | Neither would most people – and that's why a lot of them never make the journey – they just remain slaves. |
| *Voice 1* | So what's all this got to do with Jesus? |
| *Voice 2* | We'll come to that in a few minutes – right now, there's food to be enjoyed! |

## Main Course

### Second Dialogue

*Voice 1*  Well, then – what has Moses to do with Jesus?

*Voice 2*  Like Moses, Jesus called people to follow him.
He met people as individuals and called them to be part
of a community.

*Voice 1*  But Moses had already done that – they'd learnt all about
being a community.

*Voice 2*  Obviously not well enough – because they soon forgot the
really important things.

*Voice 1*  So what did Jesus do?

*Voice 2*  He called a few people to follow him, and learn from him,
and become a community again.

*Voice 1*  But . . . didn't Jesus get killed?

*Voice 2*  Yes – some people found his ideas threatening, and tried to get
rid of him. But he stuck by what he believed, and showed that
helping people to love one another is worthwhile – so
important that it's worth dying for.

*Voice 1*  So that was that.

*Voice 2*  Not by a long way! The Bible says that inside three days, Jesus had
been raised from the dead, which showed that if we believe in
something enough to make real sacrifices for it, it will be worthwhile
in the end.

*Voice 1*  It's a great story – but there's a missing element. Moses led
his people to freedom. When Jesus had finished, Israel was still
occupied, and the people were still living there. Where's the
journey to freedom?

*Voice 2*  D'you remember what I said about getting Egypt out of Israel –
all the hang-ups and fears, and greed and selfishness which the
Israelites took with them into the wilderness?

*Voice 1*  Yes

*Voice 2*  Well, the people of Jesus' day had got stuck into all that again.
He actually helped free some of them.

*Voice 1*  So what about us?

*Voice 2*  Well, think about the fears that rule our lives today fear of what
the neighbours say . . .

*Voice 1*  Fear of failure

*Voice 2*  fear of not being wanted

*Voice 1*  fear of embarrassment

| | |
|---|---|
| *Voice 2* | fear of being afraid! |
| *Voice 1* | Some people manage their whole lives on the basis of what they're afraid of. |
| *Voice 2* | Tragic, isn't it? All of us are slaves to something but the gospel says that Jesus can set us free. |
| *Voice 1* | Just like that? |
| *Voice 2* | No, not just like that. We've got to make the journey. He won't force us to – we have to agree to do it. And it's risky. |
| *Voice 1* | Like going through the Red Sea |
| *Voice 2* | and coming out the other side; |
| *Voice 1* | or even, like going through death |
| *Voice 2* | and coming out the other side. |
| *Voice 1* | The question is, how can we be certain it's going to work? |
| *Voice 2* | We can't be certain. We can only take the risk of faith – go on the journey. The important thing is that we do it together. |
| *Voice 1* | As a covenant community. |

SWEET COURSE

COMMUNION: WORDS OF INSTITUTION (2)

In the same way, after supper Jesus took the cup, saying, 'This cup is the new covenant in my blood; do this, whenever you drink it, in remembrance of me.' For whenever you eat this bread and drink this cup, you proclaim the Lord's death until he comes. *1 Corinthians 11:25-26*

THE WINE IS SERVED (IN LIKE MANNER TO THE BREAD)

COFFEE

*A light-hearted end to the occasion can be achieved, using one of the Iona dialogues – '"Eh, Jesus"..."Yes, Peter"', from Wild Goose Publications.*

VOTE OF THANKS TO THE CATERERS.

# Pentecost Service

WE CELEBRATE the coming of the Holy Spirit to bring life and freedom. A common error is to think of the Holy Spirit as filling us with excitement and power, so that we can go and change the world. Of course, there is truth in that, but it is not the starting point. The first people whom the Holy Spirit will change will be us! We then go out, enabled to meet the world as it is, and communicate with it.

# ORDER OF SERVICE

PRAYERS OF INVOCATION AND CONFESSION

Come, free, abundant Spirit of God; fill this place with the wonder of your presence; fill our hearts with your love; fill the whole church with the power of Christ. Come in all the mystery signified by wind and fire, beyond human definition, not held in the grasp of anyone, or any thought, or any programme. Come, sovereign Spirit, and move our hearts to awe and wonder. Amen

Let us now, in silence, bring before God our own failings: our smallness of mind, our slowness of response, all that burdens our consciences, and open ourselves to the freshening, purifying power of his Spirit.

*Silence*

ASSURANCE OF PARDON

If we claim to be without sin, we deceive ourselves and the truth is not in us. If we confess our sins, he is faithful and just and will forgive us our sins and purify us from all unrighteousness. *1 John 1:8-9*

HYMN        Spirit of the living God *(See Appendix)*
            *or* Come down O love divine

READING     John 20:19-23

DIALOGUE

*Voice 1*    That doesn't sound very healthy to me – or very polite, either!

*Voice 2*    What doesn't?

*Voice 1*    Jesus breathing on his friends.

*Voice 2*    Maybe, but it's a very powerful symbolic action.

*Voice 1*    Why's that?

*Voice 2*    Because breath represents life.

*Voice 1*    So?

*Voice 2*    In the bible, the same Hebrew and Greek words are used both for breath and for the Holy Spirit.

*Voice 1*    I get it! To be filled with the Holy Spirit is to be filled with life!

*Voice 2*    That's right.

*Voice 1*    But I still don't see why Jesus had to breathe on his disciples; surely, they were perfectly capable of breathing for themselves.

*Voice 2*    The point is that the Holy Spirit doesn't mean just any old life. Being filled with the Holy Spirit means being filled with the life of Christ.

| | |
|---|---|
| *Voice 1* | So, what's the difference? |
| *Voice 2* | How long can you hold your breath for? |
| *Voice 1* | I don't know, why? |
| *Voice 2* | Could you do it indefinitely? |
| *Voice 1* | Of course not! |
| *Voice 2* | Why? |
| *Voice 1* | Well, because if the air inside my body couldn't get out, it would go bad and I'd die. |
| *Voice 2* | Life's like that. If you try to keep it in, just for yourself, it goes bad and – in a real sense – you die. |
| *Voice 1* | So what you're saying is that we've got to be willing to let go of life, if we are to be truly alive? |
| *Voice 2* | That seems to be what Jesus spent a lot of time saying. |
| *Voice 1* | And doing. |
| *Voice 2* | Absolutely! And when he breathed on his disciples, it was a kind of acted parable about life in the Holy Spirit. |
| | |
| HYMN | Our blest redeemer, ere he breathed<br>*or* There's a spirit in the air |
| | |
| READING | Acts 2:1-21 |
| | |
| *Voice 1* | Well! Wasn't that spectacular! |
| *Voice 2* | Wasn't what spectacular? |
| *Voice 1* | All that wind-and-fire and speaking-in-tongues stuff. |
| *Voice 2* | Oh, that. |
| *Voice 1* | What do you mean,'Oh, that'? What did you expect me to say? |
| *Voice 2* | I thought you might say something about the breaking down of barriers. |
| *Voice 1* | What barriers? |
| *Voice 2* | Several, I'd say. |
| *Voice 1* | Such as what? |
| *Voice 2* | Oh no; you don't get off the hook that easily. You're going to have to work it out for yourself. |
| *Voice 1* | Well, give me clue. |
| *Voice 2* | All right. What was the point of speaking in tongues? |
| *Voice 1* | That's easy: so that all those foreign visitors could understand what was said. |
| *Voice 2* | So, what barrier was broken? |

| | |
|---|---|
| *Voice 1* | Oh, I see. You mean the language barrier! But that's got nothing to say to us, has it? |
| *Voice 2* | Why not? |
| *Voice 1* | Because we all speak the same language. |
| *Voice 2* | Do we? If you asked three Christian people what 'salvation' meant, how many different answers d'you think you'd get? |
| *Voice 1* | Four, I expect. |
| *Voice 2* | Exactly. We may use the same words, but we don't necessarily speak the same language. But anyway, what happened to all that stuff about life in the Spirit being for others? We've got to break down barriers not only  in the church but outside it. |
| *Voice 1* | So we've got to go out there and make everybody the same – then there won't be any barriers. |
| *Voice 2* | It's amazing how many people actually think like that. The alarming thing is that it's always everyone else that's got to change and be like them. But tell me again about the gift of tongues at Pentecost. |
| *Voice 1* | The disciples found that they were able to speak the languages of other people – and they went out and . . . Oh, I think I see what you mean. |
| *Voice 2* | The Holy Spirit didn't get rid of all the *differences*; he merely prevented them from being *barriers*. And the first people to be changed were the disciples! |
| *Voice 1* | So what's the challenge for us today, then? |
| *Voice 2* | We all have barriers that we actually rather like. And we expect other people to change to suit us. But that doesn't destroy the barriers; all our prejudices are still intact. The Holy Spirit breaks down the barriers by changing us. Not other people! |
| *Voice 1* | That makes praying for the gift of the Holy Spirit sound a bit threatening. |
| *Voice 2* | It is, if you want to stay in your own limited little world, and build walls against everyone who seems a little different. But if you do that, you might as well be dead anyway. |
| *Voice 1* | So, the choice is between isolation and community. |
| *Voice 2* | Between death and life. |
| *Voice 1* | Let's choose life! |
| | |
| HYMN | Spirit of God, O set us free *(See Appendix)* *or* Breathe on me, breath of God |

PRAYER OF INTERCESSION

God, creator of the world, let the reconciling presence of your Spirit be known where there is war, moving the hearts of all people to seek the justice from which true peace will spring.

*Silence*

Open our hearts, O God,
**and fill them with your love.**

Christ, redeemer of creation, breathe your Holy Spirit into every place. Point us to the signs of hope in cultures and faiths not our own, and reveal the love of God in every human experience.

*Silence*

Open our hearts, O God,
**and fill them with your love.**

God, creator of the world, let your Spirit move on the disorder of our existence, calling us to a life of purpose, in relationship with you.

*Silence*

Open our hearts, O God,
**and fill them with your love.**

Christ, redeemer of creation, break down the barriers we erect against others who are different from us. Fill us with your Spirit, change us and send us out to live as signs of hope and of life.

*Silence*

Open our hearts, O God,
**and fill them with your love.**

God, creator of the world, let your Spirit unite and enliven the church throughout the world, that the wholeness of creation may be signified in the unity of your covenant people.

*Silence*

Open our hearts, O God,
**and fill them with your love.**

Christ, redeemer of creation, give grace to all who are in need; heal the broken, strengthen the weak and reassure the anxious.
*(Especially we pray for . . .)*

*Silence*

Open our hearts, O God,
**and fill them with your love.**

Spirit of God, by whose power the many can be one, and in whom all creation is united in the fellowship of the Holy Trinity; come, unite us as one body, fill us with the power of love, and send us out into the world in hope. Amen.

OFFERING

OFFERTORY PRAYER

Holy God, by your Holy Spirit, you fill us with gifts beyond our imagining. Yet, in humility and love you accept the inadequate gifts which we are able to offer to you. Accept our gifts, our lives and our grateful thanks, through Jesus Christ our Lord. Amen.

HYMN    Through all the changing scenes of life
        *or* You shall go out with joy

BENEDICTION

Now go from here, filled with the Holy Spirit, to seek and serve the risen Christ in this broken world where he chooses to live.

And the blessing of God, Father, Son and Holy Spirit, be with you all, now and for ever.
**Amen.**

# HARVEST FESTIVAL SERVICE

### Seeds and Talents

THE IMAGE of seeds and harvest is here related to the parable of the talents. There are countless 'seeds' within each church, ranging from the individual skills of its members to its buildings and equipment. The question is, do we keep them safely locked away where they cannot be harmed, but cannot grow either, or do we sow them – risk them to the hostile environment where they may be attacked, but where they will have the chance to germinate?

Preparation for this service will involve conferring with the leaders of children's/youth organisations, so that they can provide items for display and presentation in the service.

# ORDER OF SERVICE

CALL TO WORSHIP

Listen now. Be still and hear. For creation takes up its maker's call. All creation draws near to God, seeks refuge from the tightening grip of winter, the winter our destruction has wrought; seeks light and warmth to revive that which we have darkened and chilled by our abuse of God's creation.

From *Advent and Ecology* Martin Palmer, 1988

HYMN      Come ye thankful people come
          *or* For the beauty of the earth

PRAYERS

Eternal God, we come to you, the giver of all good things, to celebrate the goodness of creation. Open our hearts to an appreciation of your providence in nature and an awareness of you in each other, and in the poor of the world, through Jesus Christ our Lord, Amen.

God of creation, the earth is yours
with all its beauty and goodness,
its rich and overflowing provision.

But we have claimed it for our own,
plundered its beauty for profit,
grabbed its resources for ourselves.

God of creation, forgive us.
May we no longer abuse your trust,
but care gently and with justice for your earth,
Amen.

Based on Psalm 24:1-2 from *Bread of Tomorrow* Jan Berry, Sheffield.

ASSURANCE OF PARDON

Here is a trustworthy saying that deserves full acceptance: Christ Jesus came into the world to save sinners.                    *1 Timothy 1:15*

THE LORD'S PRAYER

HYMN      For the fruits of his creation
          *or* How great thou art

READING   Matthew 25:14-29

FIRST DIALOGUE

*Voice 1*   That's a good story, but what's it got to do with harvest?

*Voice 2*   Well, tell me what you think harvest is about.

*Voice 1*   That's easy – it's about gathering in the crops.

| | |
|---|---|
| *Voice 2* | Oh, I've met your sort before – I bet whenever you read a book you turn to the back page first, to see how it finishes. |
| *Voice 1* | How on earth did you know that? |
| *Voice 2* | Let's just say you tend to give yourself away.<br>Harvest isn't the beginning of the process – it's much more like the end. Tell me how it begins. |
| *Voice 1* | Well, I suppose it begins when someone plants some seeds. |
| *Voice 2* | Well done! What then? |
| *Voice 1* | They leave them for a while, and then when they've grown there's the harvest. |
| *Voice 2* | It's obvious that you're no gardener. There's an awful lot to do in the meantime. |
| *Voice 1* | Yes, I know – all that weeding and watering stuff – not to mention keeping the slugs and snails away. |
| *Voice 2* | Right. Now look around the building and what do you see? |
| *Voice 1* | (*Looks around, with fierce concentration*) Walls. |
| *Voice 2* | Sometimes, I wonder why I bother with you! What else?<br>Is there anything out of the ordinary? |
| *Voice 1* | Oh, you mean all those paintings, and handicrafts, and flower arrangements, and tapestries and . . . |
| *Voice 2* | Yes, yes, that'll do. God gave people different talents to use – rather like seeds. They worked hard, and produced those beautiful things. |
| *Voice 1* | I get it – so it's like a harvest. |
| *Voice 2* | At last! Well, during the past few weeks, the children of the church have been using the talents God has given them, and they've been producing their own harvest from those seeds. And now they're going to show it to us. |

*Items made or grown by the children are presented at the front of the church.*
*They may simply be added to the display, but if they can be held up, described,*
*and discussed with the children themselves, so much the better.*

| | |
|---|---|
| Hymn | The best gift<br>*or* God the Creator<br>(from *Love From Below*, Wild Goose Publications) |

Second Dialogue    Harvest around the world

| | |
|---|---|
| *Voice 1* | Aren't we lucky in the developed world, to be able to produce all these wonderful harvests! I feel really sorry for developing nations, who can't produce anything. |

| | |
|---|---|
| *Voice 2* | *(After a pause)* Would you like a cup of tea? |
| *Voice 1* | What! Now? |
| *Voice 2* | Well, it's just that I know you enjoy tea, but you've evidently never stopped to think where it comes from. |
| *Voice 1* | I know perfectly well where tea comes from: India, Sri Lanka... |
| *Voice 2* | Oh, you mean those poor countries that can't produce anything for themselves. |
| *Voice 1* | Well, tea's different. |
| *Voice 2* | Really?! *(pause)* Would you like a piece of chocolate? |
| *Voice 1* | That sounds nice. |
| *Voice 2* | It wouldn't be British chocolate, though – we don't produce any. |
| *Voice 1* | Oh yes we do – it's made in Birmingham, and in York and . . . |
| *Voice 2* | But it's not produced there. it comes from another of those countries who don't produce anything! Would you like some fruit? An orange, perhaps, or a banana . . ? |
| *Voice 1* | All right, I get the point. But that's just growing things. We've been looking at the harvest of people's skills, as well. |
| *Voice 2* | That reminds me. There are some people in the church who've got some more things to show us. |
| | *Craftwork from Traidcraft is brought forward and placed among the displays. Again, if people are able to say a few words about each item, so much the better.* |
| *Voice 2* | The problem which the developing world faces is not that the people are not capable of producing anything. Often they can produce things which we couldn't begin to make or grow for ourselves. The problem is injustice in the market place. |
| *Voice 1* | In what way? |
| *Voice 2* | The wealthy nations have enormous buying power, and often inflict conditions upon the poorer nations which keep them poor. But companies like Traidcraft are changing that, by working with the poor in those countries, helping to create better working conditions, paying fairer wages, and so on. |
| *Voice 1* | Doesn't that make the goods more expensive? |
| *Voice 2* | Some people are prepared to pay more for goods if they know that it's benefiting the workers who produce them. You'll see Traidcraft items and catalogues included in the harvest display.[1] A good way of celebrating harvest would be to resolve to pay fairer prices for some of the items we buy, and support the harvest of the wider world. |

---

[1] If there is a specific Traidcraft stand in the church, indicate where it is, if a Traidcraft representative can be introduced at this point, and speak, so much the better.

HYMN    Tell out my soul
        *or* Sing we a song of high revolt

THIRD DIALOGUE

*Voice 1*    It's a strange business, farming.

*Voice 2*    What d'you mean?

*Voice 1*    Well, in what other industry do you have to take your raw
             material and throw it away, in order to produce anything?

*Voice 2*    I'm not sure I follow you.

*Voice 1*    I was thinking about those words in the Gospel according to
             John: *I tell you the truth, unless a kernel of wheat falls to the
             ground and dies, it remains only a single seed. But if it dies,
             it produces many seeds.*[2]

*Voice 2*    Oh, I see what you mean. It's an interesting thought.

*Voice 1*    A frightening one, I'd say. When the farmer sows the seed,
             there's no guarantee that it will actually grow.

*Voice 2*    All kinds of things can happen – floods, drought, pests,
             disease . . .

*Voice 1*    and even with modern methods you can't always deal
             with the problems.

*Voice 2*    You're right – it's a risky business.

*Voice 1*    But farmers are really in something of a dilemma.

*Voice 2*    How's that?

*Voice 1*    Well, if they don't sow the seeds, but keep them safe,
             then nothing will happen, anyway.

*Voice 2*    It sounds to me as though they're better off taking the risk.

*Voice 1*    So, why don't we do that?

*Voice 2*    We're not all farmers, you know.

*Voice 1*    Not literally, but we've all got seeds to sow. And I'm not
             thinking of us individually – I mean as a church.

*Voice 2*    What seeds have we got, then?

*Voice 1*    Lots. We've got the talents of the congregations,
             which often aren't used as they might be.

*Voice 2*    I wonder why that is.

*Voice 1*    Because people are afraid of getting it wrong, or because they
             think they're talents are too small to be important . . .

*Voice 2*    Or because they think that only people like ministers have gifts
             to offer.

[2] John 12:24

75

*Voice 1*    Or because they're afraid of looking pushy – all kinds of reasons – the point is that the church is full of seeds going to waste for not being sown.

*Voice 2*    Anything else?

*Voice 1*    What about buildings? Most church buildings are under-used. Often it's because of fear – if the 'wrong' people come in they might damage the place.

*Voice 2*    Sounds reasonable to me – there are some dangerous people around.

*Voice 1*    Yes, like the ones who nailed Jesus to a cross. You can't get more 'damaged' than that!

*Voice 2*    Yes, I see what you mean. And then there's our money.

*Voice 1*    Ah, well, of course we always have to be careful with money. Good stewardship and all that!

*Voice 2*    But I thought good Christian stewardship was about giving, not saving.

*Voice 1*    That's right, but it's difficult, so over the centuries, thrift has been portrayed as a Christian virtue – not because it's good but because it's safe.

*Voice 2*    As safe as leaving seeds in barns. But isn't there an awful responsibility in all this? What if we take risks with our seeds and lose them?

*Voice 1*    In the parable of the talents, the third servant wasn't punished for failing, or for losing; he was punished for not trying.

*Voice 2*    Because he was afraid of failure.

*Voice 1*    Right again. So, if we really want to celebrate a harvest . . .

*Voice 2*    We've got to go and sow some seeds.

HYMN    We plough the fields and scatter
*or* The sower went forth sowing

PRAYER OF INTERCESSION

We offer prayers for the world, especially for those places where the harvest is inadequate, even when the sowing has been great. We pray for grace to share the hunger and the hope of the world's poor.

*Silence*

Let us sow our seeds in faith,
**and trust God for the harvest.**

We pray for people in places of conflict, (especially . . .) and pray that we may use whatever influence we have, even at some cost to ourselves, to bring pressure for peace.

*Silence*

Let us sow our seeds in faith,
**and trust God for the harvest.**

We pray for those who seek to gather figs from thistles – to bring about peace through violence, social justice through terrorism, to create security by threatening and manipulating others. And we pray that we may follow, as we call others to follow, the way of Jesus Christ.

*Silence*

Let us sow our seeds in faith,
**and trust God for the harvest.**

We pray for the church, especially where it is seen as rich and privileged among the poor and deprived. God give us grace to be the body of Christ in identifying with the voiceless and the powerless in society.

*Silence*

Let us sow our seeds in faith,
**and trust God for the harvest.**

We pray for our own families and friends, and for this church fellowship, (thinking particularly of . . .)

We pray for grace to give freely of our time and resources in support of the sick, the housebound and the anxious.

*Silence*

Let us sow our seeds in faith,
**and trust God for the harvest.**

We remember the bereaved (especially . . .)

We give thanks for the communion of saints, and especially for those we love who have died. We join our prayers with theirs, and commend them anew into the unfailing care of God, through Jesus Christ our Lord.
**Amen.**

OFFERING

OFFERTORY PRAYER

We present to you, O God, the harvest of our labours, our talents and our love. Use us and our gifts for the furtherance of your kingdom of justice and wholeness, through Jesus Christ our Lord, Amen.

HYMN    To thee O Lord our hearts we raise
*or* Father, Lord of all creation

BENEDICTION

Go from here in the creative power of God, bearing the marks of the love of Christ and the life-giving gifts of the Holy Spirit. And the blessing of the triune God be with you all.
**Amen.**

# REMEMBRANCE SUNDAY SERVICE

### Reflections on Peace

THIS SERVICE is entitled Reflections on Peace. Although it is not uncommon to speak of being 'anti-war', it might be better to say 'pro-peace'. It is not that war is the natural state of things which has to be changed. Peace is the natural state, for which we and the world were designed. So the service begins from that standpoint – focused in God's promise of peace to the world. Then it moves on to see how we, as partners in creation, are called to take responsibility, and finishes by celebrating the peace which there already is in the world, and the hope of perfect peace in the future.

It is designed to be a 'peaceful' service, and includes a number of opportunities for silent reflection, following readings and meditations.

To use the service as it stands, a large globe will be required, which is capable of being separated into two halves.

# ORDER OF SERVICE

CALL TO WORSHIP

God said to Elijah, 'Go out and stand on the mountain before the Lord, for the Lord is about to pass by.' Now there was a great wind, so strong that it was splitting mountains and breaking rocks in pieces before the Lord, but the Lord was not in the wind; and after the wind an earthquake, but the Lord was not in the earthquake; and after the earthquake a fire, but the Lord was not in the fire; and after the fire a sound of sheer silence.

*1 Kings 19:11-12*

In a world full of sound and fury, God comes to us in quietness, and offers us peace. Let us prepare for worship in silence.

*Silence*

HYMN Let all the world in every corner sing
*or* A new commandment I give unto you

## PEACE: GOD'S PROMISE

READING Isaiah 55:6-13

SILENT REFLECTION

PRAYERS OF INVOCATION BASED ON 'KUMBAYA'
*The unaccompanied singing is led by a soloist, following a short silence after each prayer.*

Holy God, we turn to you in prayer, seeking a special sense, in this time and place, of your presence which is always a reality, although often unrecognised.

Kumbaya, my Lord, kumbaya,
kumbaya, my Lord, kumbaya,
kumbaya, my Lord, kumbaya,
O Lord, kumbaya.

Come, eternal light, shine into our darkness. Let your love expose our indifference, your giving of yourself show up our rampant desires, your peace shame our destructive restlessness.

Come in judgement, Lord, kumbaya . . .

Come, redeeming God, in forgiveness. Assure our forgetful and fearful hearts once more, that your only desire is to save us.

Come in mercy, Lord, kumbaya . . .

Come, Spirit of wholeness, heal the wounds we inflict on ourselves and on the world. Renew us in ourselves, in our fellowship with one another, and in our solidarity with the whole created order.

Come with healing, Lord, kumbaya . . .

READING    Isaiah 30:15-18

SILENT REFLECTION

HYMN    Seek ye first the kingdom of God[1]
        *or* Make me a channel of your peace

### PEACE: OUR RESPONSIBILITY

READING    Genesis 1:26-31a

MEDITATION

| | |
|---|---|
| *Voice 1* | What an opportunity! |
| *Voice 2* | Co-creators with God, |
| *Voice 1* | living at one with creation, |
| *Voice 2* | helping to create wholeness. |
| *Voice 1* | What went wrong? |
| *Voice 2* | Why did we throw it all away? |
| *Voice 1* | We wanted to be like God, ourselves: |
| *Voice 2* | in control, |
| *Voice 1* | supreme, |
| *Voice 2* | all-knowing. |
| *Voice 1* | How foolish. |
| *Voice 2* | As if anyone can own the air, |
| *Voice 1* | or control the jungle, |
| *Voice 2* | or harness the source of life! |
| *Voice 1* | And yet we try. |
| *Voice 2* | How foolish. |
| *Voice 1* | All the beauty of creation, |
| *Voice 2* | wild, free and magnificent, |
| *Voice 1* | here for us to enjoy. |
| *Voice 2* | And we try to tame it, |
| *Voice 1* | to exploit it, |
| *Voice 2* | and in the process, |
| *Voice 1* | we destroy it. |
| *Voice 2* | But it was created for us. |
| *Voice 1* | We cannot live without it. |

[1] This is very effective when sung in canon, dividing the congregation into two blocks.

*Voice 2*    So if we destroy it,

*Voice 1*    we destroy ourselves.

*Voice 2*    How foolish.

SILENT REFLECTION

HYMN    Dear Lord and Father of mankind

THE PEACE

    *A large globe is presented at the front.*

    *Minister*    Let us acknowledge and accept our God-given responsibilities.

    *All*    We hold the world in our arms.
    We offer it to its creator.
    We commit ourselves to a life of holding and offering.

SILENT REFLECTION
    *leading into*

PRAYERS OF INTERCESSION

    *During the silences people may simply mention people or situations of particular concern.*

We pray for the peace of the world – for a true peace based on wholeness, justice and human dignity. During the silence, let us name before God the countries and peoples for whom we are particularly concerned.

*Silence*

We pray for those communities and nations divided by the misuse of religion.

*Silence*

We pray for ourselves, in our worldliness.

*Silence*

We pray for all who, for their own reasons, stir up unrest, and seek to promote conflict.

*Silence*

We pray for ourselves, in our worldliness.

*Silence*

We pray for all whose greed, or hunger for prestige, destroys their own peace, and that of those around them.

*Silence*

We pray for ourselves, in our worldliness.

*Silence*

We pray for those we love whose lives are disrupted by anxiety, by illness, or who for any other reason are unable to live life to the full, especially those whom we now name before God . . .

*Silence*

We remember those who have died, in peace and in war, and we pray for the bereaved especially those whom we now name before God . . .

*Silence*

Holy God, we thank you for the forgiveness of sins, the resurrection from the dead, and the life of the world order to come. Amen.

## PEACE: AN OFFERING

*The globe is divided.*

DIALOGUE

| | |
|---|---|
| *Voice 1* | The world is divided: |
| *Voice 2* | by poverty, |
| *Voice 1* | by greed, |
| *Voice 2* | by the desire for power, |
| *Voice 1* | by ideology, |
| *Voice 2* | by religion, |
| *Voice 1* | by the unjustifiable plundering of its resources, |
| *Voice 2* | for the sake of unsustainable growth. |
| *Voice 1* | We must give of our resources: |
| *Voice 2* | pour into this broken world, our time, |
| *Voice 1* | our money, |
| *Voice 2* | our possessions, |
| *Voice 1* | but most of all, ourselves, |
| *Voice 2* | for the healing of the nations. |

HYMN  For the healing of the nations
*During this hymn, the offering is collected in the separated halves of the globe*

## PEACE: PRESENT REALITY

READING  Matthew 5:3-16

MEDITATION

Why do we hear so much about war,
    violence,
    destruction,
    death?

Doesn't anything else ever happen in the world?
Isn't there any peace,
    any love,
    any creativity,
    any life?

Or isn't that news?
    We don't report the commonplace,
    the ordinary,
    the everyday.

We report the unusual
    the extra-ordinary
    the different.

There's a lot of peace,
    a lot of love,
    a lot of joy,
    a lot of life;
too much to report on.

That doesn't mean we can be complacent,
    put our feet up,
    leave it to God.

But it does mean we can have hope,
    and be driven to action,
    not despair.

There's a lot of war around.
    Too much.
But it's not the natural state of things.
Peace is natural.
    And it's here.
What we've got to do
    is help it to grow.

SILENT REFLECTION

READING    Revelation 7:9-17

HYMN    Such a host as none can number *(See Appendix)*

BENEDICTION
May the Lord bless you with all good and keep you from all evil; may he give light to your heart with loving wisdom, and be gracious to you with eternal knowledge; may he lift up his loving countenance upon you for eternal peace.

# APPENDIX

# ADVENT CAROL

*Tune: Stalling Busk in 'Thirty New Hymns'*
*published by Kevin Mayhew Ltd*

From God goes forth the light of truth:
his judgement all the world shall see;
in places dark with death's despair,
his word is life and liberty.
When those we fear are pushed aside,
he chooses life among his own;
makes body, mind and spirit whole
by healing power of love alone.

His piercing light, with fiery probe,
can penetrate the prison wall;
so guilty fear gives way to hope
as deathless love transfigures all.
And we, in other ways confined,
by walls of sin we cannot see,
may hear and own his promise sure:
'The truth revealed shall set you free.'

The messenger proclaims the word:
'Prepare the way – the Lord is near.'
The one on whom the nations call
within his temple will appear.
Where sick are healed and hungry fed,
and prejudice dispelled by grace,
there death by life is overcome,
and God revealed in human face.

Among the peoples of the earth,
the Lord of hosts will take his place,
to make the poor abode his home
and simple food a means of grace.
His face is seen in hostel room,
in boarding house or cardboard home;
where cold and dark despair hold sway,
the Light of Life will overcome.

Compassion bids us face the dark,
and faith's discernment brings to sight
the presence of the God of hope,
in inextinguishable light.
So join the universal song;
proclaim salvation's daily birth:
'To God be everlasting praise,
through peace and justice on the earth!'

# MARY, BLESSED TEENAGE MOTHER

*Tune: Black Madonna in 'Thirty New Hymns'*
*published by Kevin Mayhew Ltd.*

Mary, blessed teenage mother,
with what holy joy you sing!
Humble, yet above all other,
from your womb shall healing spring,
out of wedlock pregnant found,
full of grace, with blessing crowned.

Mother of the homeless stranger
only outcasts recognise,
point us to the modern manger,
not a sight for gentle eyes!
O the joyful news we tell:
'Even here, Immanuel!'

Now, throughout the townships ringing,
hear the black Madonna cry,
songs of hope and freedom singing,
poor and humble lifted high.
Here the Spirit finds a womb
for the breaker of the tomb!

Holy mother, for the nations
bring to birth the child divine:
Israel's strength and consolation
and the hope of Palestine!
All creation reconciled,
in the crying of a child!

# LENT VIGIL HYMN

*Tune: Redcliffe in 'Thirty New Hymns'*
*published by Kevin Mayhew Ltd.*

Keep watch and pray; prepare to face temptation:
let us not seek to turn our faith to gain,
nor, for the sake of cheap self-exaltation,
divert our feet from Jesus' path of pain.

Keep watch and pray; let us not grieve the Spirit,
portraying true as false or good as ill,
but hear his word, no matter how we fear it,
and dare to live according to his will.

Keep watch and pray; Christ needs not our protection –
our good intentions bar the Saviour's way.
Our only task: to share in his rejection,
and trust to God the winning of the day.

Keep watch and pray; the mountain light enthrals us!
Here would we stay, away from pain and fears,
but from the vision fair, the Saviour calls us
to pitch his tent amid this vale of tears.

Keep watch and pray; forswear all vain ambition;
in God's good time, his purpose we shall see.
Meanwhile, in love accept the slave's position,
and share with Christ his cup of agony.

Keep watch and pray; there is no easy glory –
how premature that great triumphal cry!
Remember well the oft-repeated story:
too soon, 'Hosanna!' turns to 'Crucify'!

Keep watch and pray; the evil powers, ascendant,
with all their might conspire for love's defeat;
but from on high, in scarlet stripes resplendent,
the Christ triumphant cries, 'It is complete!'

# Do Not Touch

*The verses should be sung by a soloist, and the refrain by the whole congregation.*
*From 'Singing, Dancing Carpenter' published by Kevin Mayhew Ltd.*
*Words by Michael Forster; music by Christopher Tambling*

I met him in the garden in the early morning light,
but I thought he was the man who worked the land,
'til I heard him call me 'Mary' in his own familiar way,
and I saw the wound still open in his hand.

*Refrain:*
*'Do not touch, do not hold, do not cling,' he said,*
*'for I give you a new song to sing,' he said,*
*'and this is the word you shall bring,' he said,*
*'the Lord is risen indeed!'*

I wanted to hold onto things the way they were before,
but he said that wasn't how it ought to be.
The past is now the past, and there are better things in store,
and that is why his spirit must be free.

*Refrain:*

He's risen and he's with us in a form we cannot grasp,
and with life the universe cannot contain,
and not with nails or doctrines, or a multitude of words
will people ever pin him down again.

*Refrain:*

# FROM THE VERY DEPTHS OF DARKNESS

*Tune: Cameron's in 'Thirty New Hymns'*
*published by Kevin Mayhew Ltd.*

From the very depths of darkness springs a bright and living light;
out of falsehood and deceit a greater truth is brought to sight:
in the halls of death, defiant, life is dancing with delight!
The Lord is risen indeed!

*Refrain:*
*Christ is risen! Hallelujah!*
*Christ is risen! Hallelujah!*
*Christ is risen! Hallelujah!*
*The Lord is risen indeed!*

Jesus meets us at the dawning of the resurrection day,
speaks our name with love, and gently says that here we may not stay:
'Do not cling to me, but go to all the fearful ones and say,
"The Lord is risen indeed!".'

*Refrain:*

So proclaim it in the high-rise, in the hostel let it ring;
make it known in Cardboard City, let the homeless rise and sing,
'He is Lord of life abundant, and Christ changes everything;
the Lord is risen indeed!'

*Refrain:*

In the heartlands of oppression sound the cry of liberty:
where the poor are crucified, behold the Lord of Calvary;
from the fear of death and dying, Christ has set his people free;
the Lord is risen indeed!

*Refrain:*

To the tyrant tell the gospel of a love he's never known
in his guarded palace-tomb, condemned to live and die alone:
'Take the risk of love and freedom; Christ has rolled away the stone!
The Lord is risen indeed!'

*Refrain:*

When our spirits are entombed in mortal prejudice and pride;
when the gates of hell itself are firmly bolted from inside;
at the bidding of his Spirit we may fling them open wide;
the Lord is risen indeed!

*Refrain:*

# SUCH A HOST AS NONE CAN NUMBER

*Tune: Runciman in 'Thirty New Hymns'*
*published by Kevin Mayhew Ltd.*

Such a host as none can number,
every tribe and every race,
robed before the Lamb in glory,
gather at the throne of grace.
'To our God ascribe salvation;
glory to the Lamb belongs!'
All the saints, in one communion,
join the glad triumphal song:

*Refrain:*
*Amen! Amen! Alleluia!*
*Glory, honour, might and praise,*
*to the God of earth and heaven,*
*let the whole creation raise!*

Those who suffered great injustice,
now redeemed and glorified,
day and night their praises offer
to the Lamb once crucified.
No more shall they thirst and hunger,
no more fear the scorching heat,
for the Lamb will be their shepherd,
every need and longing meet.

*Refrain:*

See this vision of the future
put to shame the world we know!
Hear the heavenly choirs protesting
with the victims here below!
Heal the sick and feed the hungry;
set the broken captive free!
In the presence of the future,
this our joyful song shall be:

*Refrain:*

# SPIRIT OF GOD, O SET US FREE

*Tune: Spirit of God in 'Thirty New Hymns'*
*published by Kevin Mayhew Ltd.*

Spirit of God, O set us free,
let no dark fears our souls confine.
Lead us by new, uncharted ways;
unfold the Mystery divine.
We long to see, to touch, to know,
and fear the risk that faith demands;
O help us tread the desert road
that leads us to the promised land.

Spirit of God, the breath of life,
give strength to hearts and limbs that tire;
lead us through mysteries untold,
make truth and freedom our desire.
You call us on to life and hope
from all that would our souls enslave;
O may our faithless hearts not choose
the spurious safety of the grave.

Spirit of God, come like a fire
to lift our spirits in the night;
burn in the coldness of our hearts,
and lead us on toward the light.
And when, with mem'ry's distant view,
we long for some enchanted past,
then give us grace to follow him
who is the only First and Last.

# SPIRIT OF THE LIVING GOD

Spirit of the living God,
move among us all;
make us one in heart and mind,
make us one in love:
humble, caring,
selfless, sharing,
Spirit of the living God,
fill our lives with love!

# WE ARE PEOPLE ON A JOURNEY

*This hymn was originally written for the closing service*
*after a summer play-week for local children.*
*It takes up the specific ideas explored by visiting speakers each day,*
*around the general theme of 'Journeys'.*
*Hopefully, the language is such that people of most ages*
*will enjoy singing it together.*

*Tune: Battle Hymn*

We are people on a journey, moving forward every day,
with our friendship growing closer through our work and in our play,
and we learn about each other and ourselves along the way;
God's people journey on.

*Refrain:*
*Glory, glory, hallelujah!*
*Glory, glory, hallelujah!*
*Glory, glory, hallelujah!*
*God's people journey on.*

('Holidays')
There'll be sights to see and things to do, and time for having fun;
there'll be time to stand and stare, with nothing pressing to be done,
and we'll organise the journey so there's time for everyone,
as we keep moving on.

*Refrain:*

('Space')
Now, we don't know every detail that the future has in store,
but we're quite prepared 'to boldly go where no-one went before',
for we know that God is there for us, and who can ask for more?
That's why we journey on.

*Refrain:*

('Hot Places')
We may find ourselves in Timbuktu, or sailing up the Nile,
facing sunstroke or mosquitoes, or the fearsome crocodile,
but the people and the scenery will make it all worthwhile,
so we'll keep moving on.

*Refrain:*

('Treasure Islands')
There are moments when we dream about how lovely it would be
on a sunny treasure-island in the Caribbean Sea;
but our treasure is the love that God has given us for free,
so we shall journey on.

*Refrain:*

('Transport')
There are some who travel gently, there are some who must compete,
using bikes and cars and aeroplanes, while others use their feet,
but we'll end up all together when the voyage is complete,
so let us journey on.

*Refrain:*

So we journey on together with our God, who will not rest
'til the sick are healed, the hungry fed, and all the poor are blessed,
and as long as there is anyone exploited or oppressed
the journey must go on.

*Refrain:*